MAXIMIZE

M@XIM!ZE

A Playbook-Style Countdown of the Top 100 Productivity Practices

ALEX DRIPCHAK

LIONCREST

PUBLISHING

MAXIMIZE
A Playbook-Style Countdown of the Top 100 Productivity Practices
First Edition

ISBN 978-1-5445-5035-0 *Hardcover*
978-1-5445-5034-3 *Paperback*
978-1-5445-5036-7 *Ebook*
978-1-5445-5133-3 *Audiobook*

For all those succeeding, struggling or seeking to make a positive contribution to our society, I thank God for you.

Just remember, I can do all things through Christ which strengtheneth me.
—PHILIPPIANS 4:13

CONTENTS

INTRODUCTION

The 5 Second Rule: The moment you have an instinct to act on a goal you must 5-4-3-2-1 and physically move or your brain will stop you.
— MEL ROBBINS

Maybe you're picking up this book thinking, *Why should I read this? I can just read any other habit book from a laundry list of acclaimed productivity experts.* To which I'd say, you should absolutely read those books.

The beauty of this book is that it will serve as the springboard or launching point into illustrious books like *Atomic Habits, High Performance Habits,* and another 102 reputed sources. There are many ways to live a more productive life, and the goal of this book is to help steer you into the sources you'll find most beneficial; think of this book as the smallest science lab with 104 beakers, each testing various catalysts to see what'll give you a reaction.

To my productivity scholars and performance gurus, welcome! This book is most certainly for you too. While you'll see many famous habit formation, time management, and motivation techniques in here, you'll also see more than a few originals. Each section adds its own conversational, skeptic-in-mind tone with new twists and learnings, but for those craving some juicy new ideas, I think you'll be particularly excited about the energy cultivation, time mindfulness, needs-payoff, and alignment practices sprinkled throughout.

For a little about me and why I'm writing this book: I'm a bit of your everyday standout. I'm everyday in that I'm not some neuroscientist sharing thirty years of work, or CEO of a sexy, big-name Fortune 100 company. And I'm a standout—not in the societal association of the word as a star, but because I stand out by being, and thinking, differently. You can almost always find me filling my time with maximum purpose, and you can just as often find me at the gym on the treadmill…typing. I'm a big believer in that we're each here to fulfill our God-given purpose and we just need some antidotes, antifreeze, remedies, solvents, solutions, substitutions, bridge builders, and wall breakers to get us there.

While I do struggle with productivity sometimes, I am, like many of you, one who wears many hats. I'm proud to say that I have a full-time job (forty-plus hours per week), my own skill-development foundation (ten to thirty hours per week), an advisory role (one to five hours per week), and a sales coaching role (about one hour per week), all while being a husband and expectant father with a (at the time of writing this) verified happy wife (tips for that in here too), an attention-demanding pet, and good relationships with my parents, and I still see my friends as much as I'd like, all while finding a way to exercise each day and allocate eight hours to sleep. Oh, and this book is my second, and I'm lining up two more.

It may all sound like too much or someone headed toward burnout, but it doesn't have to be, and that's another reason I'm sharing these practices here. Quick disclaimer: Let me be the first to say I'm not Superman (as much as my mom likes to give me that title), and I'm not one of those ice-bathing, intense-workout warriors or any other type of extreme lifestyle liver. Nothing against the ice bathers, but I wouldn't characterize anything I do and anything I recommend in this book as physically or mentally difficult. Different? Absolutely. Difficult? Not exactly. Uncomfortable? Certainly. Unachievable? Not at all. I'm just an avid student of productivity who has kept a close eye on *many* techniques, and I want to share them in the hopes that they help you do more to carry out your God-given purpose in life. And while I am spiritual, this book is for everyone, so I encourage you to keep reading despite me dropping the G word.

This book is broken down into three sections of four: four main challenges to productivity, four main solution areas, and four sets of skills grouped by how much benefit you can expect from mastering them.

For the first four—four main challenges to productivity—I find from my readings, research, and observations that productivity challenges usually boil down to four areas: getting started, sustaining effort, finishing strong, or optimizing output.

While many practices help in multiple areas of life, I've listed each practice by the primary problem area it addresses:

Getting Started

100	94	93	90	72	64	59	57	54	43	37	32	31	30
19	18	17	16										

Sustaining Effort

98	96	88	86	84	80	76	65	56	51	50	49	48	47
42	41	39	36	25	22	21	15	14	2				

Finishing Strong

87	85	82	81	78	74	70	62	61	46	45	34	23	7

Optimizing Output

99	97	95	92	91	90	83	79	77	75	73	71	69	68
67	66	63	60	58	55	53	52	44	40	38	35	33	29
28	27	26	24	20	13	12	11	10	9	8	6	5	4
3	1												

For the next section of four—the four main solution areas—I've broken those down here:

Motivation and Alignment

98	91	90	88	87	86	85	84	81	74	71	68	56	52	51	50
44	42	37	36	35	32	27	24	20	19	18	17	13	12	4	

Energy Cultivation

99	95	92	83	78	72	53	49	48	47	46	41	34	23	15	10
8	7	2													

Time Management

94	89	79	77	75	70	69	67	66	65	63	62	61	60	58	45
40	38	33	28	14											

Habit Formation

100	96	94	93	89	82	80	76	73	64	59	57	55	54	43	39
31	30	29	26	25	22	21	16	11	9	6	5	3	1		

Unlike the crossword acronym suggested by this grouping (METH), there's nothing synthetic or harmful about these suggestions, but I do hope you get addicted to these tips and they act as a stimulant to your productivity.

Last but not least, we have four main sections of skills, grouped by how much they can benefit you. In the Commence course we refer to this as Magnitude of Impact, or MOI, and we rate each skill on a 1–10 scale of how much mastering that material can impact your life. Here I've adapted this MOI scaling to align with how important the material can be in maximizing your life.

- **Practices 100–76**: Improving Your Day-to-Day
- **Practices 75–51**: Becoming Your Best Self
- **Practices 50–26**: Optimizing Your Lifestyle
- **Practices 25–1**: Achieving Greatness

These are general themes, and not all practices will align with each theme, as final numbering is based upon each section, the importance of the practice, and the potential impact of mastering said practice. I encourage readers to not focus on whether you agree with the numbering, and instead create an action plan by writing down which practices could most benefit your life. Try to adopt more of the skills from later in the book than from the beginning, as the lower-numbered skills have the power to have a disproportionate impact on your life.

A sample action plan could be taking three practices from section one (100–76), four from section two (75–51), five from section three (50–26), and six from the final section (25–1), then reviewing those eighteen highlighted practices and choosing five to ten items at a time to implement into your life. See which work for you and which you struggle with. For the practices you struggle with, is there another commitment device, environment, accountability partner, or other mechanism to help you improve? If not, move on to one of the other practices you saved.

Now if you read my preview of all those sections and thought to yourself, *That's great, but I'm looking for even more,* well fear not, productivity junkies. I've added a fourth group of four, a "concept originality" breakdown based on what I've seen and studied. It's broken out into recapitulation, recreation, inspiration, and origination. Think of this as a continuum that spans from *That was a good way to put it* to *Huh, I never thought of it that way* to *That's a powerful expansion* and, finally, to *Wow, that's new and potentially impactful for me.*

(Artful) Recapitulation

99	98	94	84	81	73	64	59	57	55	48	47	46	43	42	41
40	39	32	31	30	18	17	8	6	3						

(Evolution and) Recreation

97	96	95	93	92	87	79	69	67	66	62	61	60	56	54	38
36	35	29	23	22	21	20	16	15	14	10	5	1			

Inspiration (from)

100	91	86	83	77	76	75	74	72	70	65	53	52	51	50	49
45	44	33	28	27	25	24	19	13	11	7	4				

Origination (First Seen Here)

90	89	88	85	82	80	78	71	68	63	58	37	34	12	9	2

Whatever the voice inside your head gets you to say, nothing is more important than the action you take. As you're reading, I want you to think of ways you can get yourself to take action. Don't focus so much on the speed at which you're reading or getting to the next number or grouping. These skills are purposely written as asynchronous so you can drop into the skill, or skills, you want to drill into most. While there will be cross-references to other skills, you do not have to read this book in order. I do suggest reading the practices sequentially for the rising or building effect it'll have on you to encourage completion, but that's a luxury I've left up to you as the reader.

Before you begin, write down five ways you're going to commit to taking action. These could be creating alarms on your phone, telling a friend, taking notes somewhere visible (e.g., phone, journal, or planner), posting to-dos on your laptop or refrigerator, etc. Whatever is obvious, attractive, satisfying, and easy, for my James Clear fans.

My Five Commitment Methods

1.

2.

3.

4.

5.

We will have check-ins after each section of twenty-five for you to reflect on items you've already taken action on and items you have earmarked for future action.

After all, the highest price we pay in life is the price of inaction.

WHEN EVERYONE ELSE IS JUST TALKING...

...BE THE ONE TO ACT

@JUNHANCHIN

100. DON'T WAIT FOR THE "NEW YEAR" TO MAKE A CHANGE

TODAY'S DATE—what is it? As you set out to read this book, let's mark down the actual date. You go-getters are welcome to write down the time too if you want. Here, I'll give you a space to document it officially:

Today's Date: _____*(and time)* _____

There's a decent chance the date above says "January (enter single digit here)." And that's OK. Hey, you bought the book, so at least it's a step. This is probably a good time to say thanks for choosing this one. 😊 The point being, many of us wait until society tells us to start a new habit, with the beginning of the year getting top billing.

The problem with waiting until our societal stimuli trigger us—or as Robert Cialdini would call it in his book *Influence: The Psychology of Persuasion*, a "click, whirr" response—is we lose a great deal of time.[1] Let's find ways to break that habit of waiting by first finding additional milestones to motivate us to start, with the intention that eventually, any day will be a good enough day to change your life for the better.

Whether it's a new month, new quarter, new job, a holiday, or—my favorite—your birthday, all these are great times to set out to make the changes you've wanted to make for a while.

Here is a list of various helpful date markers for those looking to kick something into action. While you certainly don't need one, it's nice to have a list of options.

Time-Based

- Unique days (February 29—leap day; July 2—the year's halfway point)
- New month
  New quarter
- New week
- New decade
- Equinox/solstice
- Holiday

Nature Based

- Seasons changing
- Zodiac calendar
- Solar eclipse
- Snowfall
- Hottest day of the year
- Coldest day of the year
- Most epic sunset

Life Milestones

- Birthday
- (Work) Anniversary
- New job
- Graduation
- Birth of child
- Landmark vacation
- Promotion
- Home purchase or move
- Fitness goal
- Monumental first

World Events

- Election
- Championship sporting event
- Olympics
- Monumental first
- World Cup

We will talk about artificial countdowns later on, but let's leverage the concept of a countdown here. Instead of marking when we will start something, how about marking when you expect to finish something?

Let's begin with this book. You have your start date above; now mark down your estimated completion date:

I, _____, *will finish* **Maximize**
      (FIRST NAME) (LAST NAME)

on or before _____ _____, _____
                    (MONTH)   (DAY)   (YEAR)

(Sorry, foreign readers, for the format.) ■

99. UNDERSTAND YOUR BODY'S CHRONOTYPE

ONE OF THE TOUGHEST unspoken productivity challenges is figuring out when to push versus when to relax. Pushing all the time inevitably leads to breaking, whether physically, mentally, or both. But too much relaxation and you're leaving valuable time on the table. Therefore, it begs the question: How do you strike the ideal balance between the two?

A big portion of that comes from setting SMART (specific, measurable, achievable, relevant, and time-bound) goals as well as understanding, and assessing, what will be best for you in that moment. However, a lot *also* comes down to your body's chronotype.

Your chronotype tells you when you do your best work, when you should expect a drop in productivity, and when you should wind down for the evening. Anyone who has the app RISE or the Oura Ring probably knows their chronotype quite well, and it's what I like to refer to as the *tiebreaker*. It's the tiebreaker for when you're stuck on deciding—rest or reignite?

When do you work best? If you were structuring the ideal productivity day and it ended exactly one hour before bedtime, what time would that be? If there were no schedules, what time would you go to bed and what time would you wake up?

Dr. Michael Breus has a helpful sleep chronotype test, but for a basic introduction of the four potential profiles—beginning with the early bird and ending with the night owl equivalents:[2]

- **Lion**: about 15 percent of the population. This is the equivalent of the more popularized "early bird" phrase. Overall, lions enjoy getting up early and being productive quickly.

- **Bear**: about 55 percent of the population. The typical nine-to-five commuter profile, bears follow the normal schedule peaking in midmorning and finding a lull in midafternoon.

- **Dolphin**: about 15 percent of the population. While midmorning to early afternoon is a dolphin's peak, they don't follow a typical sleep schedule and often have challenges staying asleep at night.

- **Wolf**: about 15 percent of the population. If you haven't heard of the wolf, this is the "night owl" equivalent. Wolves are productive from afternoon into the evening and often go to bed after midnight.

While schedules will get in the way, knowing your chronotype and optimizing your routine to suit your sleep profile can help you maximize your day, each day. ■

98. STRIKE A POWER POSE

DR. AMY CUDDY'S well-known research has shown that striking a power pose increases testosterone, reduces cortisol (stress) levels, and increases risk-taking; now that's quite the confidence cocktail!

While further research has not been able to reproduce these physiological/hormonal results, one thing has been proven again and again, and that is that participants *feel* stronger and more powerful in these power poses and upright positions.[3]

So what are some power poses you can employ? Here are five of my personal favorites:

1. **The French Aristocrat**: also known as the "Wonder Woman," where you put your hands on your hips and take a wide stance.

2. **Game-Winning Goal**: where you put both hands emphatically over your head, as if you just won your match.

3. **The Seated Desk Lean Back**: also known as "the Obama," where you put your hands on your head, kick your feet up on the desk (or elevated table/chair), and lean back in your chair.

4. **The Standing Desk Lean**: also known as "The Loomer," where you stand tall and wide but place both of your hands on the desk in front of you.[4] This helps maintain a high shoulder position and gives power vibes reminiscent of a gorilla.

5. **The Jacket Button**: where you use each respective arm to pull your jacket lapel to the middle to button the top button and to straighten up your shoulders and posture. This process will typically prominently display any wrist-wear too.

There are many power poses to choose from, but you'll hear people refer to the first two most frequently, as they are two of the most used, most powerful power poses. ■

97. ADOPT A DEFAULT MINDSET OF "NO"

RIC ELIAS, the CEO and co-founder of Red Ventures, has a great quote: "When you're saying yes, you're saying no to something else. Everything in life has a price."[5]

Well said, Rick, and this is especially true today when we are constantly juggling many, varied tasks, and we may lose sight of the opportunity costs that are always there and need to be consistently weighed.

In theory the constant competing priorities should make saying no easier than ever, but for many of us, it's the contrary; now it's more difficult to say no than it is to say yes.

If you can't quite get yourself to the no approach, replace your yes with a "No, not right now" or "No, sorry, not at this time" response and see if the person has a compelling reason to change your mind. If they do, perhaps you can consider a way to move it up the priority ladder. If they don't, at least you were up front and polite.

I will say this is a tip for mid-career and beyond when you're on equal footing with others position- or status-wise. For readers under the age of thirty, understand this will be a paradigm shift for you as you age and as you have more on your plate to balance.

Now if you're still worried that saying "No, not right now" will make you come across as unapproachable—or, even worse, fake—you don't have to say no, but you also don't have to say yes. You can enter the "Why don't you follow up with me so I can get a better picture of what you're looking for?" territory.

You can accomplish this by taking a small first step and making them take additional action to showcase their skill, commitment, or follow-through. Get their contact information, send the initial message, and ask for more details. If they send them in a timely manner and are earnest in their interest for your help or contribution, they will follow up. It may sound strange, and you may think 100 percent of people who asked for your help will follow up to your follow-up note, but oftentimes they do not. They get swept up by the next current of what's on their plate in the here and now and they do not respond or take the necessary action. This follow-up step ensures you can **preserve your reputation while weeding out around 60 percent of requests right off the bat.** ◼

96. UTILIZE POINTING AND CALLING

HABIT FORMATION

THE SILENT KILLER of productivity, energy, focus, alignment, motivation—all of it—is failing to call out mistakes, missteps, or misappropriations. We incorrectly assume:

1. The mistake is self-evident.
2. Someone else will point out the mistake.
3. The mistake is not a big deal.

Unfortunately, the problem is far more likely to repeat if left unchecked, and its downside risk exposure is far greater than any potential perception of us as negative beings. Bringing mistakes to light keeps us honest and vigilant. If you're worried about sensitivities or being perceived as critical, do what train conductors do: Utilize pointing and calling.

If you notice, train conductors don't wait for something to go wrong—they **proactively call out actions**. If they see someone near the platform, they pull the horn. They use their lights to signal doors closing. They make timely announcements not only to customers, but also to the rest of their team.

This doesn't work only for train conductors; it works for assembly line workers, it works for the quarterback, it works for the military, it works for surgeons—it works for anyone who has a very low degree of error allowed and where process is critical. Put in brief: If it works in high-pressure, low-error-rate, process-driven organizations, it'll work for you.

The benefits of this one extend beyond lower error rates. In a team environment, this can also serve as an energy cultivator to jolt people back into focus. After all, *boredom breeds inattention and inattention breeds lethargy*. Lethargy and errors go hand in hand as shown by a *Journal of American Medical Association* study that found fatigue was the most common reason for errors among medical residents.[6] Seems they could use a pointing and calling refresher. And some exercise. ■

95. AVOID LONG-FORM NEGATIVITY (>30 MINUTES)

EVER FEEL PHYSICALLY and mentally drained after listening to that Eeyore of a friend or that constantly negative family member who has to critique every little thing? Well, it's not just you, it's science.

It's been proven that thirty minutes of listening to or indulging in negativity decreases your hippocampus and therefore decreases your ability to problem-solve.[7]

So if you're looking to do your best work, especially anything pertaining to creative solutioning, avoid watching the news, long-form documentaries, or exposés on negative topics; reading Instagram comments; or spending time with that painfully draining family member.

I will cover negativity a few more times in this book, but for some sage advice now, let's turn to former monk Jay Shetty and work from his appropriately named book *Think like a Monk*: "To help us confront our own negativity, our monk teachers told us to try not to complain, compare, or criticize for a week, and keep a tally of how many times we failed."[8]

The monk teachers knew to teach this principle early, because negativity acts as a gateway or black hole into a deluge of despair and difficulty. It's why Jim Kwik's brain-training book *Limitless* talks about Dr. Daniel Amen's work on the need to kill ANTs: automatic negative thoughts; it's why James Altucher talks about rejecting the negativity and limitations others try to place on us in his book *Skip the Line*; and it's why Dale Carnegie starts his timeless classic *How to Win Friends and Influence People* with this (first of thirty) principle: Never complain, condemn, or criticize.

In reviewing these passages, I found they all shared another commonality: They all appear early in the book. Shetty's passage is on page 33 (out of 316). Kwik has many references to quelling negativity throughout his book, but the first appears in Chapter 2. Altucher's passage is on page 6, and Carnegie begins with his principle right from page 1. Each author talks about Recognizing, Auditing, and Minimizing negativity. In other words, we need to *RAM* negativity right away to keep it from penetrating our productivity and, most importantly, our identity. ◾

94. HABIT STACK

PEOPLE OFTEN TALK about the importance of a great morning routine, and in this book I talk about trying to dedicate at least one hour a day to routine. So how do supercharged routines get built? They get built on top of a number of habit stacks.

In a nutshell, habit stacking is this: Before, during, or after one habit, add another desired habit. This process could look like:

During my morning all-hands call, I'll go for my morning walk, and after that call is over, I'll step it up to a run.

Now that habit of joining that recurring call is accompanied by two exercises and three tasks checked off my to-do list: step count, elevated heart rate, and time outside. The day just began, and I already accomplished more than usual—that's the beauty of habit stacking.

As you can see, the cue (here, that morning call) will be definitive and obvious, and it'll help you accomplish more. The benefit of an obvious cue is not only that you cannot miss it, but also that, if done repeatedly over time, it becomes automatic. To paraphrase James Clear in *Atomic Habits*, habit is the achievement of automaticity. In the example above, the cue of one habit gets the next desired habit in queue when you habit stack. In other words, the *cue creates the queue.*

This is much of the battle as instead of having to think *What's next on my plate?* it'll be automatically primed for you. For me this is like jump rope. When I was twenty-four, I set out to make my three weakest workouts in the gym my best: pull-ups, push-ups, and jump rope. While I did improve in all three, after some medical setbacks, only one remained at a high skill level: jump rope. Now I'm not saying I'll be featured in Cirque de Soleil anytime soon, but you can tell a lot of training went into the result, and if you ask me how I do it, the answer would be boring: "I don't know—just over time it's become automatic." I don't have to think about the choreography, timing, steps, etc.—it just comes naturally, and that natural cadence builds confidence. And that's what you want to build—-automaticity in your habits—for the increase in skill, dependability, and confidence.

As Mark Manson tells us, much of life's success comes from conquering the associated negative action (e.g., going to the gym is the negative action to conquer in order to successfully get into shape).[9] I'd apply the same concept to say that much of life's success comes from *flipping what's automatic into what's intentional, and what's intentional into what's automatic.*

For example, scrolling on social media comes automatically for many of us. How can you make that a conscious, intentional, decided-upon action each time? And vice versa, getting to the gym is a random, day-to-day, time-to-time selection versus an automatic action. How can you autopilot action for the productive, and reduce readiness for the unproductive?

It's not a cliff-hanger, but rather a rhetorical question, and the answer is: _____. ▪

23. DEDICATE AN HOUR OF YOUR DAY TO ROUTINE

ONE OF THE EASIEST THINGS we can do is allow work, others, chores—L I F E—to get in the way.

When we bend our rules and limits to please others, we open ourselves up to constant distractions. And what's a world of constant distractions? It's one without flow.

One remedy to this flowless lifestyle so many are encumbered by is to have a dedicated hour to yourself specifically devoted to a routine. If this sounds like a chore, don't worry; it doesn't have to be about making your bed, showering, exercising, or any other image you've conjured up about routine. Instead, you should look to maximize your contributions by putting your time toward what author Brendon Burchard calls your Prolific Quality Output (PQO).[10] In short, PQO is what's going to separate you from everyone else. It's what's most meaningful in your life: your own personal contribution to the betterment of society. It's the legacy you want to leave. The input to assure your success.

So you see how a routine can allow for consistency, flow, and PQO, but its benefits don't stop there. By dedicating an hour to routine, you allow yourself to build multiple habits at once, or as you just saw above: You spring habit stacking into action.

A fifth and final benefit (at least for now) of a dedicated routine is it acts as an antidote to Parkinson's law, which describes the tendency to stretch tasks to fill the available time. When you know exactly how much time you have to accomplish your most desired, identity-tied tasks, you don't want to waste a minute. Whereas time may often feel like something you need to fill (e.g., at work, in traffic, or perhaps worst: waiting at the DMV), here, time serves as a powerful demarcation or countdown to what you have left to accomplish.

Quite simply, dedicating an hour of your day to routine is the **gateway maxim** or principle that opens up so many powerful practices that you'll be reading about. ■

92. ASK YOURSELF QUESTIONS FORMATTED AS ACTIVE AND CONTINUOUSLY REFLECTIVE

ENERGY CULTIVATION

AT THE END OF MY FIRST BOOK, I decided to close with a powerful question and call to action. That call to action was to reframe your viewpoint from:

Was it good? to *Was it effective?*

This simple shift gets you out of the subjective past and pushes you into the objective present. It's an immediate cure to bias as well as an immediate measurement. There are many examples of greatness or superiority that failed to persist (Apple Newton, Blu-ray, Blockbuster, BlackBerry, Google Glass, LaserDisc, Sega Dreamcast, Segway), and if they had sooner reframed from good to effective (or resonant), it could be a very different world today for not just these companies but for society as a whole. Reframing like this can be quite powerful, just as Marshall Goldsmith shows us in his book *Triggers*.

Goldsmith points out how active questions get others to think about what *they're doing* instead of what's being done *to them*. Let's take happiness for example. Instead of asking how happy you were today, which is often a summary of many exterior influences shaping our day, Goldsmith asks himself, *Did I do my best to be happy today?* The focus comes back to what you can directly control, what you're directly accountable for, and what you need to be perpetually mindful of.

Both examples of reframing harness the power of reflection, teaching us to focus on what we can continue to improve in the moments themselves, as well as realizing, and subsequently wielding, the power of knowing that life is a continuous journey of development.

If you think about it, evaluation of yourself takes any past action and makes it present because you're thinking about it now, and your goal is to see what you can learn, glean, reflect—all things that point toward how you can live a better life moving forward. Shifting to active voice will help you recognize this fact in readily apparent ways. ■

91. START THE DAY SAYING, AND VISUALIZING, HOW IT'S GOING TO BE A GOOD AND PRODUCTIVE DAY

MOTIVATION AND ALIGNMENT

FOR MANY OF US, the day starts as soon as our alarms go off and, for those who work from home, it often starts before we even get out of bed. We reach for our phones and immediately dive into our inboxes. In those five seconds it takes to scroll to your Mail icon, click on it, and see your emails refresh, your cortisol levels raise as you anticipate stress. For those who aren't careful, what those overnight and early morning emails show (or for some, don't show) dictates our attitude toward the day. Even worse, it can dictate if we have a good or bad day.

Let's rewind and play that back. You hear your alarm…reach for it. Unlock your phone to turn off the alarm. Scroll to Mail, press the icon, and the content that comes up dictates your day. **A fifteen-second process can determine our attitude, approach, and feelings for the next fifteen hours**. Talk about shortcutting—or short-circuiting, rather—your life into dangerous territory. If left unchecked, this habit can set a dangerous precedent for how you live your life.

So how do you prevent this deluge into the depressing? Set the course right from the outset. It sounds simple, but when's the last time you woke up with intentional words and actions, as opposed to autopiloting to your inbox or Instagram? Whether it be prayer, uplifting music, self-affirmations, joy-on-demand exercises, or any combination of these or other exercises in positivity, enlist as much as you can to battle against ennui and anxiety.

Bonus: Want another fail-safe for protecting against premature day labeling? *Break your day into quarters: morning, midday, afternoon, night.*

Something went wrong at your 9:00 a.m. meeting? It's not a bad day, just a tough morning. You waited forty-five minutes for lunch only to get the wrong order? Sounds like a potentially subpar midday. There was a jack-knifed tractor trailer blocking all lanes, turning your thirty-seven-minute commute into three hours? Bad afternoon. Now if all these things happen on the same day, then sure, maybe you get the moniker of a bad day, but don't label it prematurely.

In addition to premature day labeling, what's critically important to avoid is slipping into complaining. After all, while it may sound strange, complaining is a human favorite! It's relatable. It's not braggadocious. It's often unifying. It's a slippery slope into becoming part of your identity, and it's a close cousin to the Pain-Body—an accumulation of past emotional trauma—that Eckhart Tolle talks about in *The Power of Now*.

No one will admit to enjoying complaining, but I'd say a good 95 percent of people do enjoy it. I'm sometimes one of them. The key is mindfulness—be mindful of how much time you've spent complaining and how far past "getting it off your chest" you've gone. We talk about the dangerous vortexes of negativity, phones, and entertainment, and this slippery slope of complaining is another.

One activity that I'm trying now is going through my pictures to write down all of my best moments or days and inputting the date on a spreadsheet. This exercise so far has shown me that great days can happen any time, and I want to wake up and make each day, yes even that random February 4, which oddly enough has had many great moments for me, the best it can be.

Similar to how many wait until the new year to set goals, *many of us wait until holidays or vacations to expect good days.* Shed that belief. It can be hard, but call upon a higher power to help you see the best, envision the good, be optimistic about each day, and maximize mindfulness for each of the four daily checkpoints of morning, midday, afternoon, and night. ■

HAVING A
BAD DAY?

ADD SOMETHING TO
BRIGHTEN IT UP

@JUNHANCHIN

90. QUESTION YOURSELF QUARTERLY

MOTIVATION AND ALIGNMENT

SOMETIMES WE GET so caught up going from one thing to the next that we don't stop to think why we're doing it or *who we are doing it for*. It's easy to read this and think *Of course I know why I'm doing it and who I'm doing it for!* But to what degree are you certain that you could list all motivations, in order, weighted by how much they are driving you, track it over time, and prove yourself precisely accurate? This is why these questioning exercises or audits are important.

Ask yourself this question: *Am I truly living my life, or am I defaulting to the expectations, or wishes, of others?* If you can say you're truly living *your* life, you've passed checkpoint 1 and can proceed to the next question. If not, drill further. If your answer didn't start with "I want to" but rather "my (X) wants me to," "they need me to," or "I've always done," then you know you have a challenge.

Now some of you may think the frame "I want" implies selfishness. Not the case. "I want" framing could be: "I want to serve others" or "I want this to help my family with X"—you can still be centered on others but you should be able to frame anything with "I want" as the first two words. If they aren't, then you're defaulting to the expectations or wishes of others.

Checkpoint 2—*Conformity*. Are you battling against pressures to fit in? These could be set by your family, friends, or community, or they could even be your own self-inflicted pressures to conform. These habits are a bit more obvious but not necessarily easier to break. If you are battling these issues, it's important to work on what you feel called to do, as you'll do more, do it better, and do it with lasting (eternal) (Godly) purpose.

Checkpoint 3—*Money*. Are you living a life you don't love because you've grown too accustomed to a certain lifestyle and its financial obligations?

Checkpoint 4—Last but certainly not least, *comfortability*. Has the path of least resistance whisked you away into autopilot? Blink twice if you're in there! See, it's not too late. You're reading this book and checking in with yourself, asking questions like: *Is my current path something I'm happy with and finding fulfillment in? Does this current path lead to a destination I'm proud of?*

It's hackneyed for sure, but it's still equally important to say that you only get one life.

Unless you're a cat. And if you're a cat reading this book, well, then I'm both honored and impressed. ∎

89. MAKE ACTION YOUR DEFAULT

HABIT FORMATION

HOW MANY TIMES have you communicated a lofty idea, goal, dream, action, or task only to... never attempt it? We hold the idea and the mere utterance of it more sacred than actually pursuing it. We like to call upon the idea more so than find the answer. We enjoy reveling in how amazing it would be if it happened as opposed to actually pursuing it and discovering the pain that might be entailed in its pursuit. For these reasons I call it a "Lotto Motto."

The main reason I play the lottery isn't for what I think will end up being a life-changing fortune. No, it's for conversational enjoyment. It's a $2 ticket to have a "chance" at a whole different life and for that day, or those days, I can discuss freely what I would do with the money knowing I have a horse in that gargantuan race.

Once I do the math and make sure it's financially "feasible" to play, meaning the expected payout, after taxes, is greater than $576 million (1 in 288 million odds of winning, $2 ticket), I grab my ticket and get to my fun discussions. It's like buying the game Icebreaker and having just one card. Put another way, it's like paying an entry fee to partake in this game. Now, if you switched the time frame to, say, I'd find out in a few hours, I'd play a lot less. If you told me I could find out instantly if I'd won...I'd probably never play at all. The waiting is the attraction, and the imagining is how I fill the waiting.

Anyone who's played twenty questions knows this concept of imaginative time-killing well. We mistakenly carry the fun of hypothetical games over into our real lives, and the tasks that could have the greatest impact on our lives are pushed off. Procrastinated. Delayed indefinitely. Sometimes never made public, sometimes never even written down. What we must realize is indulging in the idea or discussing the never-dared dream is a false sense of security. You tell people your big idea for the "Wow" and the "That's so cool" or the "Oh people really need that," but you don't advance it, or at least not at the rate you would normally, because you're fearful of the result. At the end of the day, *it's our actions, not our intentions that progress us forward*. And with that said, I'm going to send out emails today to those who could help advance the causes I care about most. I hope you'll join me in doing the same before advancing to Practice 88. ■

ACTION

What are the three things you can do right now that'll have the greatest impact on your life? Write them down. Set aside time to do two later and do one now. Like, right now.

Action 1: _____

Action 2: _____

Action 3: _____

88. GET COMFORTABLE WITH BEING DIFFERENT

IF YOU ARE ALWAYS trying to be normal, you will never know how amazing you can be."

As someone who changed their name, chose to be mute for years following a traumatic event, and even applied for a groundbreaking role simply to wear a uniform, Maya Angelou, who penned the powerful passage above, knew about the importance of being different. And her three Grammys, Pulitzer Prize nomination for literature, Presidential Medal of Freedom, fluency in six languages, and trophy case that spans over five decades show us she also knew a lot about being productive.

Like Angelou seeking out an odd job, or reading Russian literature for fun, you too must get comfortable with the uncomfortable. The difference between you, someone seeking to better themself immensely, and those around you—many of whom will be comfortable with societal expectations, conventions, and conformities—is profound.

At first it'll be tricky, but you'll need to find ways to relish the "what are you doing" looks or discomfort inherent in sticking out. Experiences tell me to push past the discomfort for three reasons:

1. Not anywhere near as many people are paying attention to your difference as you may think.
   a. (especially in major cities)

2. If they do take notice, they aren't thinking about it anywhere near as much as you may think.

3. It's not always bad news.
   a. I have many encounters with people stopping to ask me—with fascination—about working on the treadmill, reading a book while walking down the street, or any other nontraditional task I do. Often they are interested in learning how they can do it themselves. Those positive interactions occur far more often than any negative encounters. The risk of long-lasting effects from a negative encounter are

nearly infinitesimal, while the opportunity from a positive encounter is nearly infinite.

b. *The critics will sit silently while the connections will speak sonorously.*

So step out and dare to be different. It just might help you strike up a conversation and relationship you otherwise would never have, and in that way it's perhaps the greatest organic networking tool at your disposal.

To quote another someone who accomplished a lot in her own style: "In order to be irreplaceable, one must always be different." Thank you, Gabrielle Chanel, for what can serve as this practice's self-affirmation. ◼

87. USE DUTY AND LOVE AS MOTIVATORS; AVOID FEAR AND SUCCESS AS PRIMARY FACTORS

MOTIVATION AND ALIGNMENT

THIS SECTION IS an adaptation from one of my very favorite authors, Jay Shetty, and his book *Think like a Monk*. Reading these four motivators, I—and many of you, I imagine—had an inner monologue progression that sounded like this: *Makes sense*, *Obviously*, *Duh*, and—*Wait, what?*

Duty as a motivator—that makes sense. Love—yes, obviously, that's a great motivator. Avoiding fear—well yeah, duh, no one wants to be afraid. Avoiding success—wait a minute, what was that?

Let's take a step back to analyze this one.

Fear, while it is something we aim to avoid, is a powerful motivator. We fear negative consequences like getting yelled at, scolded by the boss, and laid off or even downright fired. However, fear as a motivator erodes. If you slip up here and there, you may remain motivated by fear to avoid that feeling, but when complete and total failure occurs—and you realize you're still A-OK—you're no longer afraid or at least dramatically less impacted by fear and/or those employing it. This shows us that fear only has power over us when we give it power. And fear is no match for faith, as Norman Vincent Peale shows us in his acclaimed *The Power of Positive Thinking*.[11] If fear erodes over time, or suddenly, and if fear cannot stand against faith, then fear is a flawed, consumptive source of motivation.

So if you're not afraid of something anymore, what's next on the motivation continuum? Success.

Striving for greatness and gain propels us forward, but *how about when we have enough?* Or when we realize there's more to life than seeking our own personal gain?

That's where duty and love play a part. Doing something for a greater good that you're strongly connected to is not only eternal, it's also replenishable daily. The only issue with duty, at least in a societal interpretation of the word, is it's often interpreted alongside self-sacrifice, strenuous effort, and potential peril. What's the first association you have with duty? Officer on duty maybe? Or perhaps an image of a military veteran. Even the term "civic duty" draws up this sense of *needing* to do something versus getting to do something. Duty has the potential to slowly wane.

Now for this highest form of nonconsumptive and continuously strengthening source of motivation, we finally get to love. The more you do something you love, the better you feel. It's like the endorphin rush and clear-headedness we get from exercise without the pain and sweat. Now you know the deep thinking behind the emphatic, overused phrase "Do what you love and you'll never work a day in your life." It truly is the strongest motivator available to us. ■

86. DON'T LET VICTORY DEFEAT YOU

MOTIVATION AND ALIGNMENT

STOP AND ENJOY the moment, but don't revel in it too long.

Remember, life keeps going; don't stop.

There's plenty of room at the top but no place to sit down.

Chances are you've heard one, if not all, of these phrases. Why is that?

Well, we as human beings tend to overestimate our abilities and feel comfortable with what we've accomplished early on. We refer to what we're trying to do as what we're doing, and we call either ourselves or others "experts" in a field well before the 10,000 hours mark Malcolm Gladwell imprinted in our minds or even before the 7,400 hour study average Anders Ericsson references.[12] Think about it: How many people do you know who would label themselves as experts long before they've earned the title?

This phenomenon, known as the Dunning-Kruger effect, is full of both amusing and sad studies of people's overconfidence in their competence. One study found that 80 percent of people rated themselves as above-average drivers.[13]

One of the quickest ways to fall victim to victory is to let prior success lull you into a state of complacency (or even worse, a state of overconfidence/illusory superiority) and delude you into thinking you're doing better than you actually are.

For those positivity gurus and affirmation lovers (I am one too) complaining, "This is too harsh," allow me a quick note. I'm not saying to start kicking yourself and knocking yourself down constantly. All I'm saying is to find ways to be objective. Whether you can do it yourself or need some outside advice on how to do it—get objectivity. Instead of looking at the negative that you're perhaps not as good as you think you are, be confident in your pursuit of bettering yourself. After all, it's a rarity, as most people continue to either (a) delude themselves, (b) wallow in their self-pity, or (c) take small, cherry-picked opportunities to seek feedback. But this is not you. You're consistently finding ways to improve. To get better. To push yourself. To pursue new heights. To advance your field. To advance your industry. To advance humankind.

Now that's one hell of a narrative to write and one hell of an antidote against the arrogance or achievement attitude others are afflicted by. ■

BONUS

Need one more push over the edge to prioritize this practice? There are many studies that show people judge your skill or capabilities more by your peaks than your troughs. So, if you keep pushing further and excel more, you're elevating your position in people's eyes and further safeguarding yourself in case there are more troughs than peaks.

85. PRETEND THE PERSON YOU ADMIRE (OR DESIRE) MOST IS WATCHING

WHILE EGO IS SOMETHING we often refer to negatively or as something we need to keep close tabs on, it is still one strong motivator. Just ask Sigmund Freud. Use this to your advantage by creating everyday opportunities to act how you would in your peak moments. Better yet, go where the people you admire are and operate there. Entrepreneur and noted author Patrick Bet-David in his book *Your Next Five Moves* took this a step further by having someone create a photo of all the people he admired to motivate himself to strive for a level of greatness he could relate to and be motivated by daily.[14]

To expand upon this concept—take the work you're doing right now. Imagine that with your utmost attention, drive, and focus, it will change the world forever.

Your actions are so important that they will change the course of human history.

Your work knows no bounds. Your genius cannot be grasped; it breaks the bounds of normal human performance. You're Rain Man counting through seven decks of cards. You're Lucy reading 6,378 pages of research in a few seconds. You're Steph Curry making 105 three-pointers in a row. You're in the zone. You're a voracious learner, a spectacle people are captivated by. A marvel people are inspired by. **Your focus has others in awe**. Your heightened state, or "madness," is immediately assumed as prodigious.

Get lost in the flow that comes when you're trying to impress someone you care about and watch your concept of personal performance skyrocket. ■

84. SET GOALS AT 105 PERCENT OF YOUR CURRENT CAPACITY

MOTIVATION AND ALIGNMENT

ONE OF MY FAVORITE THINGS about Peloton is its ability to get you to push beyond your limits by showing you your personal best pace in real-time every step—or pedal, rather—of the way. When we set goals beyond our current capability, we push ourselves further, and as David Goggins reminds us: When we think we cannot continue, that's really only 40 percent of our fully utilized capability. In other words, our body's warning signal or check engine light comes on once we've hit 40 percent of our peak. While both frightening and encouraging, this figure illuminates for us how much we can progress and build…safely.

Now you may say, "Well, awesome! If we are so unknowingly conservative, let's set goals at 250 percent of our current capacity! If we know just pushing past the initial 'can't go on' layer is 40 percent yet we interpret that as 100 percent, a quick math exercise shows us that 40 is to 100 what 100 is 250. Ipso facto, 250 percent is what we should set goals at." Well, for many reasons that's not realistic. For starters, 250 percent of what you currently do is a daunting task and will scare off many from even attempting to accomplish their goal. Secondly, those who do go for 250 percent are likely to either burn out or break down, and neither is what you're looking to achieve. And third, if this is a goal that you've iterated several times, there may not be enough runway to improve 250 percent. For example, if you're already running a four-minute mile, then a 3:48 mile, or 5 percent better, is something you can accomplish; however, a 1:36 mile, or 250 percent improvement in your time, is not something human beings can accomplish—or at least not for the foreseeable future. ■

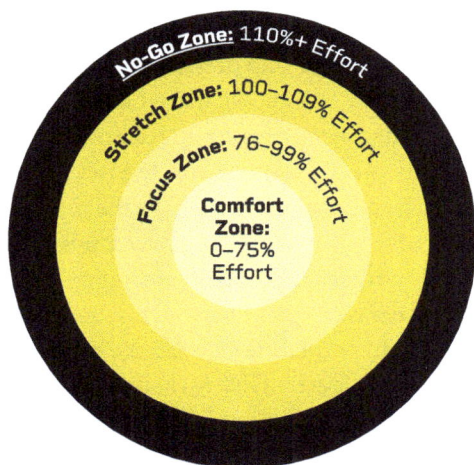

No-Go Zone: 110%+ Effort

Stretch Zone: 100–109% Effort

Focus Zone: 76–99% Effort

Comfort Zone: 0–75% Effort

83. WEAR YOUR BEST ATTIRE

ENERGY CULTIVATION

FOR ANYONE WHO'S SEEN the movie *Forgetting Sarah Marshall*, you'll remember Peter's ex-girlfriend calls out his laziness by saying, "Peter, you wore sweatpants for a week straight." While you can write it off as a movie quote, its humor is rooted in truth. It tells us that the quickest way society identifies someone who's lazy is by their appearance. While it is a shortcut, since there are plenty of mangy or disheveled productive people, it's one that still holds a lot of power. Why does it hold such power? Well, it's because comfy clothes are a signal to ourselves as well. Much like our environment, which we'll discuss later, clothing is often accompanied by specific activities. And comfy clothes are what we put on when we're lying around the house, sick, or going to bed. So the comfier the clothing, the more we have to battle against the brain's implicit association of relaxation and diminished productivity. Put simply, we need to battle the desired default we have toward something simple.

When you're battling your least productive times, sometimes you need to look like a million bucks to feel the same way. In a post-COVID-19 world it's very easy to forgo dressing up, but it's still worth giving it a shot. It may seem silly, but it's worked for me more than once.

Why does dressing up work? Think about the association of nice attire; it's often accompanied by some of your finest, most desirable, and most memorable life moments. The big presentation, your friend's wedding, that big new client business meeting—chances are more than 50 percent of the times you're getting dressed up, you're preparing to be at your best, whether it's socially or professionally. Like Superman donning the cape, we throw on the suit jacket. Dressing up is a priming activity and one we should use to our advantage. If you need a little extra pep talk: You spent all this time getting ready; you might as well make the most of it!

Now for anyone saying how correlation isn't causation or saying they work well in their casual, comfy clothing—I understand and empathize with that statement. My point here is this: Sure, you can be productive in your loungewear, but why battle through the brain's default desire to inhabit your typical loungewear activities? Make it a point to at least wear something you'd be comfortable in and confident about if seen in public when endeavoring to get something done. ∎

82. SHORTEN YOUR TIME TO ACTION AND CHECKPOINTS

"We are A–Z thinkers, fretting about A, obsessing over Z, yet forgetting all about B through Y."
—RYAN HOLIDAY, *THE OBSTACLE IS THE WAY*

WE'VE ALL HEARD that good things take time, but what many forget is why: It takes time for others to get back to you. Meaning you need to hit send quicker than you might think, because it could take weeks to hear back from someone. Don't hamstring yourself and think that the timetables others have should be yours too.

I've seen great concepts and ideas fail and many others struggle because the internal timelines weren't aggressive enough. It would be lots of talk and strong thoughts only to meet again next week to discuss the same items again and how we should record these ideas or take notes. The following week these great ideas from week one would finally make it into an email, perhaps alongside another good idea. The fourth weekly meeting falls on a holiday so no meeting that week, and week five is when we finally take action. What could have been four to five days to action ends up being four to five weeks. Don't let this be you.

The big reason this happens is *people confuse motion with action*. They think talking is doing. They think dancing around something is the same as dancing. Tiptoeing is the same as moving forward. Crawling is the same as walking. They are wrong.

When it comes to our pace, we're often biased in overestimating how much we're doing—much like the Dunning-Kruger effect we discussed earlier—when in reality we should be turning up the dial. Again, as Ryan Holiday points out: If we're walking, we should be jogging. If we're jogging, we should be running. And if we're running, we should be all-out sprinting.[15] ∎

ACTION

For two weeks, track your time in each category:

TIME SPENT						

Stillness: Time spent doing nothing (e.g., watching noneducational TV, surfing the web, phone scrolling, playing video games, etc.)

DAY						
1	2	3	4	5	6	7
8	9	10	11	12	13	14

Stagnation: Time spent thinking about doing something (thinking about applying for that job)

DAY						
1	2	3	4	5	6	7
8	9	10	11	12	13	14

Motion: Time spent talking about doing something (what you're going to do for that job application)

DAY						
1	2	3	4	5	6	7
8	9	10	11	12	13	14

Action: Time spent actually doing or producing something (applying for the job)

DAY						
1	2	3	4	5	6	7
8	9	10	11	12	13	14

Progress: Time spent advancing your cause (e.g., interviewing, screening for the job)

DAY						
1	2	3	4	5	6	7
8	9	10	11	12	13	14

Breakthrough: Time spent on in-the-moment successes (e.g., job offer, negotiations, contracting, etc.)

DAY						
1	2	3	4	5	6	7
8	9	10	11	12	13	14

81. TIE YOUR PERSONAL PERFORMANCE TO CAUSE(S)

MOTIVATION AND ALIGNMENT

OK, READY to move forward?

…are you sure?

In some of our section countdowns you'll find many items alluding to success as a potential derailment. Yes—success as a demotivator. Don't let victory defeat you. Avoid success as a form of motivation—we come to it from time to time. And while there are some alternative suggestions given in each section, here's one section devoted to those who want to keep success as a motivator, but to extend it beyond its typical…connotation.

The following principle gets you to focus on something bigger than yourself, keeps you incentivized when you have "enough," and perhaps most importantly, keeps you hungry. The word "hungry" as it is associated with hard work in a job or career is what I'd describe as one of the greatest compliments to someone's work ethic, yet one of the strangest observable phenomena.

If you think of someone who's hungry for success you probably think of a young hotshot recent college grad (I know a few, in case you're looking) or of a poor or struggling person eager to get themself into a better situation. In my observations, that hunger is found in the majority of the intern or recent college grad pool and often among those less than six months into a job, and then it's mostly nonexistent outside of those three categories. Interns, early-career professionals, and new hires. When it comes to groups of people, that's about all I've seen.

Now I'm not saying people get lazy—there are plenty of workaholics and proud ten-plus-hour day-ers—but people itching to grow, to succeed, are few and far between. Instead, what happens is most folks realize that they've settled into a comfortable life, and they know what they need to do to keep that comfortable life they've grown quite fond of.

So how exactly can you break this seemingly societal inevitability?

Enter Brendon Burchard.

Burchard has studied thousands of high performers and broken down their success composition into six habits or principles, à la Stephen Covey's *The 7 Habits of Highly Effective People*. The one I'm alluding to here is Burchard's third principle: raising necessity.

Burchard talks extensively about how to stoke the fire and drive a hunger for achievement centered on one's identity, obsessions, sense of duty, or urgency. He encourages one to "Look beyond your individual performance or feelings and connect with a reason to be your best for others. Find somebody or something worth fighting for. If you stoke the necessity…you'll hit high performance faster and stay there longer."[16]

So next time you feel your hunger being satiated and your comfort levels and safety net start to cocoon you, think of what you have an unusually strong connection to and interest in. Whether it is a cause, charity, person, religious reason, or group, harness the power of that desire to help to take action and move that thing forward. ■

80. SAY OUT LOUD (TO YOURSELF) WHY YOU'RE OPENING YOUR PHONE

IN GREEK MYTHOLOGY, there's a story about how Zeus gave a beautiful box to the first woman on Earth. He cautioned her not to open the gift, but her curiosity was too strong and she opened the box, unleashing all the world's ills. This story of Pandora and her (gift) box is much like our phones. We may come in with good intentions, but our curiosity overwhelms us and supplants our desired goal. An important note here is it's not some sort of personal deficiency. It's not like it's an individual "you" problem. The gravitational force toward entertainment is so strong that it has its inventors themselves feeling guilty over their work.

Johann Hari tells us many of these powerful stories in his book *Stolen Focus*. Stories about Aza Raskin, the inventor of the infinite scroll, going to great lengths for social responsibility with technology following the application of infinite scroll. Tony Fadell, coinventor of the iPhone, waking up in cold sweats that this invention had helped create a "nuclear bomb" capable of blowing up people's brains and reprogramming them. But no story is more powerful than that of James Williams, the Google strategist who posed a seemingly positive question to an audience of tech designers that yielded a surprising result. The question—"How many of you want to live in the world you are designing?"—elicited zero raised hands. It really feels like we live in a world where people are incentivized to profit off of others' decline and misfortune; it's our modern-day version of (subconscious) drug dealers peddling drugs of inattention and technological reliance. And unlike the drug trade, next to no one is abstaining.

If you think it's not a big problem, let's do a quick exercise. Take a quick look at your phone right now. Paying no mind to the borderline infinite content you can consume on YouTube or Google, how many apps would you estimate you have? Give it a good look. Maybe a minute or so to come up with an educated guess.

Three hundred thirty-nine. That's the number of apps on my phone as of August 2024. Sixty-four on my home page alone, thirty-seven on page 2, not including the recurring bottom four again. Forty-five on page 3 (plus the static four), ninety-five on page 4, thirty-two on page 5, thirty-seven on 6, and finally thirteen on page 7.

And we wonder why we can't stay on task. Worse yet, we can't stay on task, and then when we do check back in to full presence, we often feel guilty about the time lost. To replay that back, *we lose the time twice*: once when we scroll and a second time when we lament the loss.

So I'm here to not only say, "Don't feel bad," but to also suggest you should start being vigilant about using the voice inside your head, or under your breath, to specify why you're opening your phone.

Some good news is we are already primed to do this whole "talking to ourselves" phenomenon. Take two-factor authentication. We usually receive some six-digit code we need to input into our other machine to log in. What do you do when this happens? Well, you likely say it repeatedly to yourself as you toggle from one machine to the next. Harness this "talking to yourself" when it comes to your phone. *What do I want to do? I want to see if I have any emails from Joanne about that upcoming event she's running.* Or OK, *what am I going to do? Open Gmail—look for Joanne's email. If nothing—close phone.*

This is just one way you can start to combat your phone's endless entertainment vortex.

This brings me back to Pandora's box. The little-known part of the Pandora's box tale is it's not an entirely bad story. After all the ills and evils are released into the world, out comes one especially powerful force for good: **hope**. And just like our modern-day Pandora's box, there's hope for us too, and that hope lies in our very next practice. ▪

GUIDED ACTIVITY

Need an accelerant or aid to help you accomplish phone intentionality? Organize your phone's "pages" by theme. For example, have one page of apps for finance, one for your career, etc. Organize them in order by how much you think each is beneficial to your legacy. The most beneficial apps should be prominently displayed where you look most often. The essentials like hotel check-ins or online banking get their own space, the detractors are grouped into one catch-all gray box and labeled as such, and for the super detractors or time vortexes, you can put those inside a gray box and onto a second page within the box so it is not visible from your initial screen. This will help you scroll through your phone and land on one of the desired areas. After all, scrolling LinkedIn could land you your career-making role, whereas doomscrolling Reddit...well, let's just say it's a lot less likely to offer anything life-changing.

79. USE APPS TO YOUR ADVANTAGE

While there are many time-sucking apps, there are several productivity-enhancing ones as well. Here are fifteen of the top ones for individuals to try for themselves and watch the hope come flowing out of their entertainment box:

(Pomodoro) Timers

- **Focus Keeper** is a pomodoro-based (twenty-five minute sessions) timer.
- **Session** (according to reviews) appears to be a slightly more elevated experience than Focus Keeper because it has not only a pomodoro technique basis but also some helpful analytics around focus, distraction, breaks, mood, and more.
- **Forest** is a clever, gamified way to keep focus that rewards each completed time window (without distraction) with a tree, with the goal to build a…well, you get it.

Time Limiters

- **Opal** is intention-setting for your phone. This makes it a great pair to Practice 80.
- **Freedom** is a timed, kick-you-off-the-internet app. It allows you to limit or block certain websites or categories of sites (e.g., shopping).
- **ClearSpace**, my personal favorite, is an amazing way to limit phone use and even has a direct tie to physical fitness.

Sound Apps

- **Tide** does sound, meditation, and timers, so it's a good all-in-one sound app if consolidation is important to you.
- **Brain.fm** allows you to use existing soundscapes (e.g., coffee shop) or create your own options to help you focus.
- **Endel** is an app focused on AI soundscapes that are designed to match your circadian rhythm and environment.
- **Brainwaves**, an app I've used intermittently for years, has a bit of everything for sound: It has binaural beats, nature sounds, and frequencies for really any situation you could think of.

To-Dos and Reminders

- **Taskade** is an AI productivity app that visually starts from scratch but it works from the get-go with AI agents to help you through your productivity challenges and tasks. Other than timers, I haven't seen it stumped, so it is pretty impressive.
- **Todoist**—which happens to be the number one recommendation from my AI chatbot in Taskade—is a well-regarded deadline and priority task management app.
- **Remember the Milk** is a more niche app than others listed here, but it's especially helpful if you have trouble managing and remembering reminders and to-dos.

Multibenefit Apps

- **Fabulous**, perhaps the most expensive of the apps, is also the most inclusive, expansive, and engaging I've seen. You can tell it's designed well just by the fact it opens with a questionnaire, advances to a pick-your-price "free trial," and moves to offers to pay every two months. Its extremely well-thought-out abandoned shopping cart methodology is something every company should use. I just wish it harnessed its guided tutorial approach a little more.
- **Superhuman**—If you are looking for help managing email, Superhuman can clean up, automate, guide, and anything else you need to dig out of the area where most of us spend most of our time.

While any of these apps can be helpful on its own, don't forget about one that comes free and built in: your Screen Time app. This is a good place to start for indicators of your productivity. ■

DISTRACTION
~~DISTR~~ ACTION

@JUNHANCHIN

78. CREATE "ARTIFICIAL" DEADLINES AND COUNTDOWNS

STRANGE, RIGHT? To see the word *artificial* without its sentence partner "intelligence."

Creating artificial—or, rather, manufactured—deadlines will inspire a level of action and hyperawareness of time that we rarely get to experience.

I used to employ this practice regularly during my first few internships when I was not only hungry but also keenly focused on how others saw me. I probably went overboard on this during my internships, but I used to set, and impose, deadlines on myself by the hour or before certain day markers. This often looked like: I'm going to finish this report before lunch, before the next meeting, before Pam gets back from lunch, etc.

What I noticed during this stretch was that my focus was next level. I was not only very productive, but also truly indistractable. While it might not be practical for folks nowadays to go an entire day without picking up their cell phone or responding to a single text, this deadline concept is one to use to your advantage where and when you can. Next time you're struggling to finish a task ask yourself: *If I were completely focused with no downtime at all between tasks, how long would this take? OK, and how long will it take me to realistically set up my environment to allow this to happen?* Combine those two numbers and there's your deadline. Say it's forty-five minutes of focused work and five minutes of environment setting. You now have fifty minutes to finish said task. An important disclaimer here, from what I've seen, is this: When we employ inspiration or motivation to be our catalyst, it is effective for an individual task or set of tasks, but not as a lifestyle. The risk to one's mental health is too high. And while we used the word *artificially* earlier in this section as a positive, we don't need to see its bad side: We don't need anyone artificially amplifying their own stress and anxiety, and a countdown mentality applied too broadly in life can do just that.

Now that we've established the limitations, let's discuss another way this semiartificial countdown could be applied: life events. Anything you have coming up on an exact day that you're looking forward to, use it as your backdrop and backstop. This could be a friend's wedding, an upcoming vacation, or if you're me right now, a child on the way. The one single, far-out dead-line gives you time to accomplish much while keeping you more present and cognizant about the unstoppable force that is time. Personally, I've noticed for myself and for others that time passes by about two times faster than we think. What felt like ten days ago was actually closer to twenty days, and what felt like twenty days ago was actually forty. It's why so often people say, "I can't believe it's been so long!" The less we move around, less we enjoy, less we do, the greater the multiple. Think about your most recent trip—I bet you can recall all (five) days pretty well. You have clear locations, memories, enjoyable dynamics, etc. Now go back to your last week of work—can you tell me with similar accuracy what you did? Barring a series of big presentations, confer-ences, or events, probably not. This example shows us we are more time blind than we notice, therefore intentionality of time tracking becomes paramount to living an action-oriented, productive life.

When I reflect on timelines, I find that the more defined and shorter the blocks for check-in used, the more thankful I am for this exercise. It goes without saying that these check-ins are invaluable in setting, and checking on, SMART goals. Deconstructing a big goal or a long timeline is imperative, and doing so in short (but not rapid) ten-, fifteen-, or twenty-day markers for something like pregnancy has been valuable. It's one thing to say I'm going to do X by Y date, but when Y is something that's greater than three weeks away, it's good to set at least one check-in to see if you're progressing at the expected rate. ■

77. CHECK YOUR PHONE: TIME SPENT AND PICKUPS

TIME MANAGEMENT

LET'S DO THIS one together. Right now. iPhone users, at least.

Go to your settings—click Screen Time.

Click See All App & Website Activity, scroll down to Pickups, look at your number for last week by scrolling left. Check your number for yesterday too.

Who had fewer than 150 pickups yesterday? Solid. 125? Good. 100? Nice. 50? Amazing. Spending less time on your phone starts by knowing where you're at throughout the day. Therefore, I recommend checking your pickups two to five times a day to see your progress and to make plans to actively reduce your reliance upon your phone.

If left unchecked, a *phone is our adult blankie*—it's a default, go-to comfort catch-all for all moments. Boredom? Grab the adult blankie. Anxiety, fear, loneliness? Blankie. Discomfort in the unknown? Blan-kie. It's an autopilot and a time filler.

If you begin by checking where you're at five, ten, and fifteen hours into your day, you'll be able to break this habitual time-filling and have Screen Time serve as an anti-autopilot, checking you back into presence. Next time you have the urge to pick up your phone, just look around the room, train car, subway station, etc., and observe our societal digital dependence. Simply stopping and looking around heightens your awareness. Take a second to be proud you're (working on) breaking the cycle. You even have my permission to judge others and feel just a tad superior for a split second. 😉

Now that we've tackled presence, and hopefully your technological dependence and its accompanying anxiety, let's scroll back up to Screen Time and try to cure time blindness. Here the time is important but so is the category breakdown. Look at the results—are these results you're OK with? Sometimes Google Maps needs to be on for an hour, or Teams or Zoom needs to be open for that call you joined when your computer was down or, even better, when you were outside on that walk during the latest all-hands call.

Evaluate your Pickups and Screen Time on a day-to-day basis and give yourself a score of how you did on your phone utilization. Once you've done this for a week, consider coming back to it on a weekly basis to note your improvements. ■

76. KEEP A VERY VISIBLE PROGRESS TRACKER

"Of all the factors that have been studied, the strongest known force in daily motivation is a sense of progress."
—ADAM GRANT

LADIES AND GENTLEMEN, please welcome to the page, Snapchat.

For those who are like me and never indulged in the effervescent and youthful app—Snapchat is a social media app that employs more than 5,000 employees and is valued at over $14 billion. Founded in 2011, it is, at the time of writing this, the fourth-fastest company to reach a valuation of $10 billion, accomplishing that extraordinary milestone in just 5.4 years. That's faster than Facebook, Twitter, Dropbox, and a whole slew of other massively successful companies. So how did they do it?

Well, that's an answer for a much longer section than this, but in my opinion, Snapchat's true brilliance is in the fact that, over the years, I've heard many people say to me, or just in my vicinity, "I have to keep up my Snapstreak!" For the satisfaction of seeing a daily chat streak continue, and unlocking new emojis, people would drop everything to get on Snapchat. What a way to keep up user engagement.

While you might not have the idea, time, dedication, luck, and skill to start a streak-spreading epidemic, you can easily create simple commitment trackers. Whether it's a gold sticker or, if you're like me, a jar of marbles, use something that tracks your progress and "streak." Feed those trackers daily so you can see them build and, more importantly, so you can see and comprehend the magnitude of loss should you miss that "daily feeding."

An essential key to ensuring this works as well as it can is to put in the extra effort to label that tracking system. I've used a jar of marbles for a few years now, some labeled with my goal and some unlabeled. The labeled jars have always reached greater volume than the unlabeled. It may sound elementary and artistic, but the labels serve a bigger purpose as a written reminder to you, your roommates, and your visitors of what you set out to do. Without that label, and a prominent display, it's just a jar we forgot to put away with some things left over inside. It goes from being a powerful signal to others of your dedication and commitment to being easily seen as junk and, even worse, as unimportant to you. By not putting in the extra effort, you implicitly signal to your brain that it's just an empty jar and not a measurement of commitment. To maximize your commitment measuring devices, here are five steps to ensure your progress tracker is successful:

1. It's *attractive* (something you like and find enjoyable that's presentable to others).
2. It's *prominently displayed* (clearly visible for others to see on a daily basis).
3. It's *easy to update* and *keep updated*.
4. It's *clearly labeled* and *tracked*.
5. It's something you *take great pride in* (both as a vessel and as a daily habit).

A quick bonus to ensure the days don't stack up against you: Keep a separate pile next to your measuring device for each day you miss. Ensure this is both unpleasing to the eye and inconvenient (e.g., marbles are spilling onto your desk) so you have yet another reminder to keep on track. Not only do you want to see the desirable jar grow in volume, you also want to make sure the unsightly piles don't become a mess. ■

SECTION CHECK-IN

My Three to Five Potential Practices:

1. _____

   _____

2. _____

   _____

3. _____

   _____

4. _____

   _____

5. _____

   _____

75–51

BECOMING YOUR BEST SELF

75. ASSESS YOUR PRODUCTIVITY CHALLENGES

DO YOU STRUGGLE starting, sustaining, or optimizing your work?

In other words—is it a motivation, energy, or focus issue?

While it could be all three, it's more likely that any productivity issue you're facing is rooted specifically in one of these, so which is it?

Let's first tackle issues around starting.

Starting can be a procrastination, priorities, or motivation(s) issue. If it's a motivation issue, have a contingency battle plan ready. It's inevitable that some days you will face low motivation, so what do you do if you know an issue is likely to pop up? You plan for it. Ask yourself: *How will I face the days when my motivation is low?* Give yourself ten to fifteen things to ensure you can battle back against your motivation stagnation. Here's a preview of mine: Get into the library. Put my phone on pomodoro (focus setting). Put on my repetitive rhythms playlist if I need creative energy or my no-words playlist if I need to do some deep thinking or reading. Come prepared with my green tea, bottles of water, and/or focus supplements.

If it's an energy issue: assess. How did you sleep? Are you exercising enough? Where can you implement a nap or exercise before or during your work so you can sustain that work? Do you have a long enough time block for those solutions? If not, could you try some quick interventions in similar categories, like calisthenics to get your heart rate elevated and brain flowing, or a meditation to provide a sense of calm and relaxation? If neither the full energy cultivation exercise nor its abbreviated version is an option, assess your third plan of action. Perhaps a stimulating conversation with a friend on the phone or colleague in the hall, or watching a comedy skit during a quick break.

If it's an optimization issue, expand the number of checks you do. Beyond sleep and exercise, check:

- ✔ Your water intake
- ✔ Your scents—rosemary, peppermint, lemon
- ✔ Your foods—salmon, turmeric, greens
- ✔ Your time of day—Focus on your chronotype. Don't waste precious time doing dishes, watching TV, etc. Align your day. Aligning is optimizing.

Now that you've thought through which part of the process you struggle with, have you thought of the triggers that throw you off course? As Marshall Goldsmith tells us in his aptly named book *Triggers*, "a trigger is any stimulus that reshapes our thoughts and actions."[1]

Perhaps you have your time of day, location, food, and music all picked out, but there's a trigger that's pulling you away from your (best) work. Audit those triggers.

When it comes to documenting or auditing your triggers, don't think about just the frequency at which things pull you away from your work, but also the length of time. For some, social media is a frequency issue fracturing their attention and preventing them from flow, but for others it's a time suck—taking up thirty minutes or longer at a time.

For me, that time suck is trip planning. Sometimes I'll look for a hotel and an hour later I'll end up with a list of a dozen options across three different trip dates. Since trip planning often starts as a seemingly harmless act and ends up running a significant portion of my day, I need to be cautious about when I begin trip planning; it's an activity that needs a full runway of time. This brings us to timing as the ultimate priority: If you know you have trouble stopping something, structure your day to have time for this task either before an activity that has a firm start time or after the day is completed.

Trying to do a task when you know you have work you should return to makes the whole process troublesome, as it is both anxiety-inducing and cognitive-dissonance-increasing. It induces anxiety because the time you're spending on your pleasurable task means it's time you spent not working. And conversely, once you do go back to work, there's the constant feeling of being pulled to either resume the pleasurable task or just think about it. If you're worried you won't be able to eliminate your triggers, fear not. It's not necessarily about eliminating your triggers all the time; it's more about planning for them and asking yourself: *When can I give myself the time, place, and mental headspace to enjoy this break unperturbed?* ■

74. APPRECIATE TIME AS PRECIOUS AND FINITE

WE TEND TO GET ON with our days on, well, a day-to-day basis. Sleeping, eating, working, laundering, Netflixing, scrolling until…it's over. Another day in the books. The problem with "another day in the books" is that it's stagnating. It's not building, it's not setting production, advancement—fulfillment—into motion, and it's certainly not compounding its potential impact. Before you know it, another day is another week, another week is another month, another month is another year and then…poof…it's gone. One less year you have to make an impact on others. One less year you have—or had, rather—to contribute to leaving the world better than you found it.

Considering our first fifteen years aren't very much our own as we develop, and our last fifteen years may have their physical and/or mental limitations, that leaves us with around fifty reliable years to maximize our life and its positive impact on others. In the example above where one day left untouched charted the path for a year of nothingness, you just squandered 2 percent of your maximized life. Slowly, subtly, and unconsciously wasteful. How does that feel to hear?

You can call it dramatic or call it a gross exaggeration, but there's one thing you can't call it, and that's untrue. This happens to many people. Ever not see someone for a year and then catch up with them over coffee or lunch that year later and think: *Same old (Joe). Nothing ever changes with (him).* Well, those folks who live their comfortable life never pushing themselves further, never giving back to others, never expanding their horizons, is that really a maximized life?

You reading this passage right now has unlocked a level of heightened awareness for this example of (Joe) to not be you; well, not today at least. But what can you do to ensure the busyness of life doesn't carry you down a current of unconsciousness? Insert the three T's checkup. Maybe not every day, but endeavor for an end-of-day check-in at least once a quarter by asking yourself:

If I were to (tragically) die today, would I be comfortable with:

- What I *told* others?
- What I *tried* to accomplish?
- What I *trained* to be? ■

73. KEEP A HABIT SCORECARD

PERHAPS IT IS no surprise to readers who know the productivity publishing world, but the habit scorecard is another James Clear favorite. The principle gets at: Do your actions, and your desired actions, cast a vote for or against your identity?

This principle extends beyond just the actions within the field you're pursuing, but into bettering yourself as a whole. For instance, you can't have activities, hobbies, or even relationships that are the antithesis of your chosen area. It might seem rudimentary to say the pope can't be a volunteer for Planned Parenthood, but what are the areas in your life where you hold competing ideals? I know I personally held two for a long time—attempting to be very fitness-focused while also running a food blog centered on pizza and cocktails wasn't exactly the easiest thing. Sometimes it's more than just the glaring opposites or the challenging impediments, but it can also be the aspiration of doing too much. Even Michael Jordan learned he couldn't play baseball and basketball at the same time. And for basketball enthusiasts like myself, thank God he went back to basketball.

For those wondering about the frequency at which you should look into your own habit scorecard and what to be focused on, focus on having the pluses outweigh the minuses each day. Even on the break days you should be becoming or building toward your desired identity, and gaining more than what you're losing in a break, vacation, or any other form of nonadvancement. And to avoid burnout, keep in mind that rest in and of itself is not a loss or a negative, so don't think that rest is counting against you. It's what you're doing while resting that could set you back with dangerous competing beliefs. Enjoying a break and indulging in a well-earned treat is one thing, but letting it outweigh your advances is another. As James Clear tells us: "Missing once is an accident; missing twice is the start of a new habit."[2] Here, breaking desired identity once is an indulgement; breaking desired identity twice is the beginning of a new pattern of competing ideals. ◼

72. TAKE RISKS

I'M IN THE MIDST of challenging myself to step outside my comfort zone in small ways every day for a year.

It's not always easy, but one thing I have noticed is all the items I would typically be self-conscious about (say, dancing in public) I just say to myself, *Oh, that'll be my "outside the comfort zone" for the day!* What would normally be a relentless moment of crippling anxiety is now an accomplishment. Another box checked for the day!

This may not sound like a lot but as someone who's spent a lifetime trying to impress others and do my best at every little thing, this is a real game changer. For decades I would spend time worrying about tasks or activities others wouldn't think or worry about. Most of the time, these activities would even be considered fun! For example I have on more than one occasion spent days worrying about shooting hoops with friends—*What if I do poorly? Even worse, what if I do poorly and never get another chance to play with them, and they only think of me as the kid who couldn't play basketball?* The anxiety got to me and often robbed me of many of life's enjoyable moments.

This new mentality of celebrating a tick box in my outside-the-comfort-zone challenge gets me to push past the discomfort. I get to mentally "blame" it on a task I have to complete, as opposed to deciding if I want to opt in and then subsequently worrying about failure or the judgment of others.

You may ask yourself, *How does this translate to greater productivity? Or: I see how it gets you to do different things, but not necessarily more or better?*

Well—it's often the hardest, most uncomfortable tasks that we push off until they are no longer relevant, no longer available, or no longer possible.

To envision this more clearly, imagine you're at an event and you want to introduce yourself to the famous event speaker. You're nervous so you continue to prolong and procrastinate until...they've left. They're in the cab and on their way to the airport, only for you to never see them again. Damn. Missed life opportunity.

However, if you say to yourself, *Oh, this can be my daily outside-the-comfort-zone challenge!* No matter what, you're checking a box and patting yourself on the back. No matter the outcome, you are accomplishing something. That not only means you're much more likely to go introduce yourself, but it also means taking a lot of pressure off that engagement.

Long story short, stepping beyond your comfort zone helps you expand and grow as a person, it serves as an anti-autopilot, and it acts as a great liberator of mind, body, and spirit. ◾

COME ON! IT GETS EASIER AS YOU GO!

OBSTACLE

ALEX DRIPCHAK & @JUNHANCHIN

71. COMPLETE A DO, DON'T, OR DELEGATE ASSESSMENT

EVERYTHING IN LIFE has an opportunity cost, and some are bigger, and more hidden, than others. Figure out the items you don't want to spend time on and make plans to mitigate or eliminate them altogether.

For me, there's no bigger time suck than maintenance and DIY work. First off, my brain seems to turn off when I see assembly instructions, and secondly, I have no interest in it. This means for me, I'm avoiding home ownership. Buying a home often involves a lot of maintenance, upkeep, and weekend projects. Since these are areas I'm neither skilled nor interested in, home ownership would be a detractor from my purpose. Alternatives of condos, townhomes, or apartments give me enough flexibility to find the best situation for me so I can sidestep this normal societal progression.

For many, another societal progression or expectation is having children. While a great thing for many, it's not for all. And getting back to our section on why you do what you do, you shouldn't let anyone, outside of maybe your significant other, greatly influence or sway you into choosing this giant, constantly demanding life event. Perhaps it's not a binary question of yes versus no; it could be a question of how much or how many. For instance, you could decide to have fewer children so you can focus more fully on what God has given you for a purpose. And if God's purpose is for you to have five children—amazing! Point being, don't let society or family tell you how to live your maximized life.

Now that we've covered the big, societally expected decisions, let's move to the hidden large time commitments in life. An unassuming one is travel: Fewer trips can buy back a lot of time. While vacations are much needed, trips, in my definition, require a lot more planning and, therefore, time. So perhaps instead of a multicity and multiflight trip, you can take a vacation to a familiar favorite destination. That alone can gain you back dozens of hours to spend on your purpose or on those tasks we've labeled as your PQO, courtesy of Brendon Burchard.

Now, when it comes to the more readily solvable tasks in life, we have the following Do or Delegate activity. This will help you manage more common, recurring tasks that eat up time and that you can pay someone else to help with—things like doing your taxes, mowing the lawn, tutoring your children, cleaning the house, etc. ■

Activity: *Housekeeping*

Time you want to spend: *30 minutes/week*

Time you do spend: *3 hours/week*

Delta: *2.5 hours/week*

Opportunity cost of lost time: *Very low, low, moderate, high, very high*

When this time is lost relative to peak productivity/energy: *No energy, low energy, moderate energy, high energy*

Financial cost to fill gap: *Very low, low, moderate, high, very high*

Implicit cost to fill gap: *(0–10 on level of importance and impact, where 0 is no impact/not important and 10 is highest impact/highest importance).*

For: *Wife is happy—8; Clean, productive environment—5; More significant focus on other things—6*

Against: *Financial cost—3; Calendar restraint—3*

Implicit net cost: *(Add points for, subtract points against) 19 – 6= +13, in favor of gap filling*

Decision (Go/No Go): *Go*

Have you ever thought about the time commitments involved in five of the most time-consuming areas of life? It can be easy to get swept up in a moment and make a decades-long or even lifelong decision without giving it much thought. The following chart can help you map out what you'd like to prioritize in life. Those living in a high to very high chart location perhaps aren't going to have the time to manage multiple jobs or many social engagements, while those in the low to no category have a lot of additional time to explore a second job, or perhaps a new hobby.

	Very High Time Commitment	High	Moderate	Low	Very Low/ No Time Commitment
Living	Multihome ownership, flipping homes, managing properties	Home ownership	Townhome, condo	Co-op, apartment	Renting
Children	3+ children	2 children	1 child	Adopting adolescent child	No children
Pets	Dogs	Dog	Cat	Fish, plants	None
Hobbies	Coaching	Woodwork, crafts, DIY	Volunteering, blogging, learning a language	Chess, gardening, fantasy sports	Yoga, birdwatching, golf
Travel	Frequent flying (weekly+)	Monthly travel	Semiannual to quarterly trips	Annual trip, annual vacation	Local excursions

70. ENSURE ENERGY-TASK ALIGNMENT

IF YOU'RE FEELING a little slow, or if you know multitasking is unavoidable, you should focus on the mundane, simplistic tasks that you know you can accomplish. And on the opposite end of the spectrum, if you're firing on all cylinders, you should pursue your most impactful endeavors.

Now this may sound simple, but we often get stuck in a societal construct, an old, ingrained habit of "I'm stuck and I need to get unstuck," which leads to "I need to fight this long and hard." The problem with that is we end up spending so much time battling to perform versus performing, and once we do finally get over the hump, we are producing at a rate that falls far below our norm. While you get an A+ for effort, you get a D where it really matters: output. So next time you're trying hard to get anything done, perhaps put aside the executive summary and opt to input some tasks into Salesforce. Administrative tasks do have a time and place, and it's when you're too tired or unfocused to do the things that matter most.

To better understand energy–task alignment, or more aptly named focus–task alignment, a quick rundown on brain waves may help.

The lowest level brain waves (below 4 hertz) are delta waves, and for a healthy adult, they are most commonly linked to sleep and deep states of relaxation. They are essential to rejuvenation and restoration.

Next are theta waves (4–8 hertz), and these still exist sometimes in sleep but also in deep daydreaming. They are essential for creativity but difficult for attention.

The bridge brain waves—between the creative, daydreaming theta and the higher-production beta—are alpha waves (8–12 hertz). Alpha waves help calm the body down and exist mostly in awakened, relaxation states.

The most wide-ranging of state of mind associations (12–40 hertz) are beta waves. The right amount of beta waves helps us focus, and their stimulating effect also helps with memory and problem-solving.

The highest or fastest brain wave is the gamma wave (25–100 hertz). As the wave associated with the fastest brain activity, it is responsible for cognition, learning, and information processing.

In review and in order there are: delta, theta, alpha, beta, and gamma waves. It's the beta and gamma waves that are primed for optimal workloads and theta waves that are primed for ideation and creativity. If you're having a hard time producing the most aligned waves for the task at hand, binaural beats can help focus your brain for the desired state. While much of the research supports the efficacy of binaural beats, it's worth pointing out that they work best as an amplifier or enhancer as opposed to a state changer, so look to them more as a boost next time you're seeking energy–task alignment. ■

69. UNDERSTAND EACH TASK'S PRIORITY AND DUE DATE

TIME MANAGEMENT

THROUGHOUT THIS BOOK there's a focus on doing more, doing it better, and optimizing to do it more consistently. But how about doing the right things? It sounds so simple, but the whole "work smarter, not harder" catchphrase is memorable for a reason. When it comes to priorities, the new saying can be "work clearer, not nearer or dearer."

Without checking in on priorities we're likely to work on what we like best, on what we're best at, or for whom we like best. You could work ten hours straight on a project for your boss and still miss the mark. How is this possible? Well, perhaps that project isn't needed until next week, while the one your team leader gave you is needed in two days. To make matters worse, the work you got done ahead of schedule doesn't even get recognized because your boss is unlikely to review materials a full week in advance, as the week prior has its own fires to put out and tasks to tend to. What first seemed like a most impressive win ends up as an unappreciated miscue.

So how do you avoid this situation of explanation, rationalization, and frustration?

By creating a check-in system.

At task intake, find out the priority level and due date. If it's something that's going to take more than two weeks, plan a check-in call at the halfway point to ensure you're on track with expectations, and use this opportunity to subtly check in on the due date. Perhaps the definitive need-by date is now a "nice to have." Or the client relayed that a key decision-maker is on vacation, therefore the meeting will be moved to the following week.

Secondly, you should be sure to capture two dates: the internal preferred time and the drop-dead, need-by date. You should be working to deliver slightly before the internal preferred, but this exercise will usually have people rethinking how much prep time they need or, more likely, how much prep time they'll be able to have due to internal schedules and time conflicts. Someone may have said they want it two days before the due date, but Jane is out that whole day at a client, so the requester realizes that having it Wednesday EOD instead of the original ask of Wednesday morning is just fine. This extra day allows you to overdeliver elsewhere and ensure you're working on the right things at the right time.

This whole process not only ensures alignment, but it also does something else very powerful: If you know something is due by a certain time, it lights a high-temperature fire under your ass. When I wrote for the newspaper in high school and college, I realized nothing is quite as invigorating for an assignment as a deadline two hours after you cover it. I carried this mindset over into my first two internships and it lit a fire under my ass that I still try and replicate.

One extra word of caution: Be careful not to rush your work and risk a submission rife with errors; use that fire to be diligent about your editing, proofreading, and formatting too.

Now for those who have the freedom to choose their activities and whose performance is measured by long-term results and not the day-to-day (e.g., sales, entrepreneurs, etc.), I've put together the following model. Those familiar with the Eisenhower Matrix will see the shift from measuring urgency and importance to measuring impact and likelihood, and a move from four boxes to a twenty-first-century adaptation with nine boxes. The Eisenhower Matrix is fantastic for sorting through a list of tasks you already have in front of you that you are (most) likely to do; this activity's focus is to determine if these tasks are worth doing, as well as to open your mind to additional activities that can have the biggest impact on your life. I encourage you to come back once you've finished the book to see if you can find at least five 1s, five 2s, and five 3s to add to your life. In other words, create your own (productivity) 5-5-5 deal. ■

Pursuit Decision-Making Nine-Box Matrix

	Impactability	
6 High/Low Taking Side Job Loosely Connected to Identity Capital	**3** High/Medium Launching New Idea in a Job that Would Result in Promotion	**1** High/High Final Stages of Interview, Contract, Book Deal, etc.
8 Medium/Low Taking Job Disconnected from Identity Capital	**4** Medium/Medium Running Event at Your Job	**2** Medium/High In Process/Warm Lead to Purpose or Economic Driver
9 Low/Low Avoid at All Costs: Video Game Levels	**7** Low/Medium Pitching Article to Newspaper, Instagram Semi-Influencer	**5** Low/High Cold/Cool Outreach to Investor, Online Job App at Dream Co.

Probability (vertical axis) — Impactability (horizontal axis)

68. BREAK THE ALWAYS-ON MINDSET

ONE OF THE MOST dangerous parts of technological innovation is speed. Processing speed, time to market, innovation speed—all this speed has created a fast and furious culture. This mentality has penetrated our most sacred place: our mindset. We are constantly checking our phones, computers, emails, and social media DMs to see if anyone has reached out. And (God forbid) if they haven't, we are just a buzz or chirp away from frantically picking up our phones to see what it is. If you get past the constant checking or the buzzing and chirping, you don't escape the simple fact that you would want someone to respond to you as soon as possible, so what do you do? You treat people how you want to be treated, right? After all, that is the mindset we've grown up with. Point being, whichever of these three mentalities binds you to your phone, the fact is, we're held hostage by them.

Break free by beginning to use ClearSpace or another application like it to minimize the amount of scrolling, lingering, or otherwise unnecessary entertaining we do so often. Let others know if they need you quickly to try calling, as you'll have your social media and text messaging sitting behind a technological gate. This gate not only doesn't notify you of incoming messages, but it also adds layers of complexity to delay you from even opening apps. If there's one thing we, as modern, technological people, have a harder time battling than our phone's imprisoning effect, it's waiting. Attention spans, constant choices, and information overload translate to: Why wait? Just go do something else.

If you're having trouble breaking this "always on" mentality, realize that it extends outside the bounds of technology and into the workplace—heck, even the home. We as human beings have a propensity to exist in and around others, and without a barrier, like a closed door or visible pair of headphones, people will just begin talking to you. We are so accustomed to breaking from what we're doing to respond to each other that it'd seem rude not to reply, unless we're visibly unreachable. This realization drives many of us to feel like we're always half-listening to others, relentlessly ready for conversation.

So how can you turn this "always on" mindset off? Ask yourself: *Where can I exist completely without distraction? Where can I achieve totally pure and clear thinking?* Listed are the places I've come up with so far that provide such a feeling of having your own personal, impenetrable thinking bubble:

1. Running a bath or in the bathtub while it's running
2. In a working steam room
3. Behind or next to a waterfall
4. In the shower
5. Next to a white noise machine
6. In a soundproofed room
7. Cooking with the fan on ◾

67. TRACK EVERY SINGLE ACTIVITY YOU DO IN A DAY FOR THREE TO SEVEN DAYS

TIME MANAGEMENT

SIXTEEN WAKING HOURS in a day may seem like little when you're constantly autopiloting and scrolling, but it's actually quite a lot. If you don't believe me, try writing down every single activity you do for a day.

You'll see when you input every activity (yes, even including those taboo-to-talk-about ones) into a calendar that we do a heck of a lot of lingering, waiting, daydreaming, and doomscrolling. However, you shouldn't let this realization scare you. Instead, this tracking will unearth a sort of zen hyperpresence previously unknown to you. Put another way, could you tell me the exact number of minutes you don't maximize each day? I imagine for 99 percent of us, the answer is no, so the hyperpresence you'll uncover when doing this exercise will open up new ways for you to combine tasks, habit stack, temptation bundle, and more. In other words, this is a gateway activity. And it's one I've only completed once. Here's what I realized from that experience:

You know that feeling you get when you're rushing to an important appointment or meeting? That feeling of being acutely aware of every minute, every thirty seconds, heck, even every ten seconds that pass?

That's what you tap into when you track every activity.

Now if you also feel some anxiety at the very thought of this supreme time awareness, I'd suggest starting this activity on a weekend that has few obligations, when productivity is viewed as a plus, as opposed to a weekday when lack of productivity is viewed as a minus or loss. Go into this activity realizing how time blind we are and that our minds often capture what we do on a half-hour or hourlong basis, and not with this every-minute mentality.

To ease that jump from not tracking to tracking, start with writing down what you did every five or ten minutes of the day, before going to an every-minute or two-minute basis. After all, ten minutes is six potential activities per hour for sixteen hours, so it equates to nearly one hundred activities. Of course, you could just get into a few flow states and make the time tracking that much easier. 😊

Now some of you may say, "If I wrote down every activity, I'd lose a ton of time simply on documentation!"

To minimize time spent on writing everything down, try to seek out longer activities you can stay on task for and jot down your distractions in shorthand before adding to your calendar. Personally, I realized later than I care to admit that opening a single calendar item and periodically jotting down time stamps was far simpler than constantly opening and closing new calendar slots. Even better than one calendar invite was tracking everything in a running note on my phone and emailing it to myself later that night to add to my calendar for recordkeeping and reflection.

While this practice comes with many disclaimers, I found it quite helpful, and I'm eager to try it again. Are there any accountability partners out there willing to tackle this James Altucher–recommended practice with me? ■

66. PUT ALL TASKS ON YOUR CALENDAR

TIME MANAGEMENT

THIS IS ONE of the few tips I aim to practice every day. Some may ask, "Why? Isn't it just a giant waste of time?" I find that putting your tasks on a calendar gives you a reliable log of what you've accomplished while forcing you to stay on task, both in the sense of personal ownership (not wanting to have holes, gaps, or uncomfortable blank white spaces on your calendar) and veiled outside accountability (your calendar will show as full for those looking or for anyone going back to check calendar logs).

This practice extends further, as it also helps you journal later. I know how frustrating it is when I'm frantically trying to remember what day I did something or when I sent that last file. While search functions are getting better, they're still not always reliable, especially when it comes to a document search.

It may sound strange, but calendaring also helps you revisit prior conversations and initiatives. Meeting entries serve that purpose for many, but meetings are often labeled generically—especially recurring ones—and oftentimes you won't be the creator of that meeting, making it challenging to leave your notes on someone else's invite and hard to track the timeline and follow through from idea conception to presentation to actualization.

One of the outsized impacts I've noticed from calendaring is having date and time stamps on ideas, strategies, inventive approaches, and more. Knowing when these back-of-the-napkin ideas and transient thoughts took place helps me identify when to expect more and gives me insight into leading indicators of successful, creative thinking. Perhaps it was that account analysis that fueled the idea to create an award recognizing top prospects. You won't know if you're not tracking it. (It was, by the way.)

I'd recommend calendaring as you go or soon after an activity is done. If you want to do it in advance, mark your time as free or tentative. You shouldn't block yourself from opportunities to meet or help others or in any way come across as less collaborative or team-oriented, so keeping a calendar note open while you're free to jot down what you've been able to accomplish is a good strategy. As always, try and keep these windows short, thematically linked, energy-level aligned, and appropriately drilled/single-tasked. ■

65. USE INCREMENTS OF FIVE, TEN, AND FIFTEEN MINUTES ON YOUR CALENDAR

TIME MANAGEMENT

NONSTANDARD MEETINGS, meaning not thirty- or sixty-minute meetings, are an adjustment. Heck, just to get Outlook to understand you're not defaulting to the standard is a pain. But here's the hidden gem you'll find: People are more receptive to unusual and shorter meetings.

They'll appreciate the efficiency, they'll enjoy the break, it's almost guaranteed to be a conversation starter, and you'll end up looking, and being, more productive. These are just five of many reasons for breaking the calendar default using nonstandard meeting length, and there's really only one against it: It's not the norm.

Moreover, by properly incrementing your calendar for your own work, you'll accomplish more. If your task is "send email to Jane" and you know it only takes ten minutes, it's likely to fall victim to Parkinson's law, or the phenomenon that a task expands to fill its time allotment. All of a sudden, that email took thirty minutes, and worse yet, you feel accomplished because guess what? You checked it off your to-do list—go you!

This may sound rather innocent, but it gives you false dopamine rushes and makes that dopamine hit too readily accessible. Before you know it, your definitions of the words *success*, *productive*, and *work* have been falsely interpreted and, if left unchecked, negatively impacted forever.

This is why I refer to Parkinson's law as the silent killer. A sedentary lifestyle can lead to heart disease and be a silent, unforeseen killer; Parkinson's law is similar, but worse.

Most people know sitting around constantly isn't good for them, but accomplishing a task? Well, that's a good thing! To draw a more apt analogy: Parkinson's law is like a savings account—having money in savings is shown as a good thing in our society and is lauded as an accomplishment, but letting money sit in a savings account rather than spending or investing it will net a loss due to inflation.

Don't succumb to Parkinson's law, don't default to the norms, and maybe don't keep too much money in a savings account. 😊 ■

PUTTING IT INTO PRACTICE

You may be asking yourself, How do I know how long something is supposed to take?

Think of a task you do on a recurring basis—something you do weekly or even daily. Time how long that activity takes when you're at your peak focus, another time when you're at your average focus level, and a final time when your focus is low. This range will not only show you the importance of maximizing your peak periods, but it'll also give you the timetable you need to calendar in the future and truly know if you're falling behind (and by how much) when your energy and focus are low.

64. MAKE DEFINITIVE PLANS WITH OBVIOUS CUES

HABIT FORMATION

WHEN PEOPLE TELL ME they're struggling with adhering to a desired action they'd like to make into a habit, the issue(s) usually comes down to one of three things: commitment, impatience, or visibility. Since commitment and impatience are covered in other practices, let's tackle this third, and more complicated, challenge: visibility.

Visibility here refers to making sure your desired action is front and center in your mind, your planner, and your literal eyesight. Personally, I've wanted to do a better job addressing my health, but I've historically done little to make it front of mind. My planner has sections for my job, mission, passion project, and spirituality, but it doesn't have a category for health. And so, like many others, I address my health on a reactive basis. Worse actually, it's on a "only if on fire" basis. And sometimes, to my detriment, it hasn't even been addressed when it's on fire. So, it's clearly not on my mind, and it has no spot on my planner. That means I've failed the first two visibility checkpoints, so how can I ensure I hit the third checkpoint: visual cues?

For starters, I set alarms on my phone to book appointments and agree to snooze them until it's booked, avoiding the easy way out of just pressing stop.

Second, I leave myself a written note on the refrigerator. You may say, "Wait, I rarely stop to consume the content that's on my fridge." In that case, for those readers simultaneously taking action while reading, let's put the sticky note on the computer.

For my forward thinkers and real go-getters, you may say, "That's good, but it's easy to tear down that note and get to the million items that lay behind that screen waiting for me." So what should you do?

Let's put that reminder note on the driver's seat. For me, and perhaps for you too, this might be the perfect place, because during my car rides, I'm usually indulging in personal items like catching up with family or listening to music; after all, the possibilities are limited by the fact that, well, I need to be driving. This means it's the perfect time to reach out for that appointment or get more clarity on medical options.

So to go back to our practice title of making definitive plans with obvious cues—what's the definitive plan? Call the doctor on my next car ride. Obvious cue? A sign or sticky note that's preventing me from driving to my destination. I'd say that's more than obvious; it's quite literally an obstruction.

Beyond the steering wheel sticky note, what are the definitive plans, obvious cues, and most readily actionable places and times you can be harnessing in your life? ▪

63. PAUSE YOUR ENTERTAINMENT FOR 4+ MINUTES

IN 2019 THE National Science Foundation witnessed the merger of two stellar-mass black holes that resulted in a black hole 142 times the mass of the sun. That's 47,286,000 times the weight of Earth and the second most powerful force observed—second to the entertainment vortex available from our phones.

While I exaggerate for dramatic effect, a streaming platform sucks us in like a black hole and keeps us weighed down like Thor's hammer. So how do you break free?

Next time you can't seem to break free from a show—try pausing the show for four-plus minutes and getting up to go do something else outside of the room. Maybe fold some laundry. Do some dishes. Check your emails. Go to the store.

Are you still thinking about the show? Or did your mind jump to something else already? If it jumped to something else, you don't need the show, so continue without it.

If it's something you find you're still curious about, try to resist the urge to watch for another five minutes. After that next five minutes, think of it this way: If the urge to watch isn't eating away at you—where you're constantly thinking about how you just have to find out, right this very second, what's going to happen—then you don't need it.

If your instant-gratification monkey is high but not tremendously desperate, a less harsh decision-making process would be to see how you feel when you ask yourself: *Can I come back to this tomorrow?* If that answer isn't a resounding no, then it's a yes. Yes, you can come back tomorrow, and you should.

Now I say four minutes or longer to ensure it's longer than a bathroom break or phone call that we may be accustomed to during a show and its commercials. Yes, I'm looking at you, Hulu, and those fellow Hulu customers too lazy, budget-conscious, or principle-standing to upgrade.

If you can't bring yourself to get up off the couch, don't think that gives you a free pass; pause it anyway. Oftentimes it's the comfort of the couch and not necessarily the show that's keeping you there, but when the TV is left on, the couch and TV team up to be an unstoppable force. So break up the dangerous duo and at least just turn away from the TV, if not read a book. See how you feel. If you're really that tired, maybe a nap will do you good. If you're not, then you'll realize it's time to get up. ∎

LOOK OUT! SIDESTEPPING THE SIDEWINDERS **75**

62. SCHEDULE DISTRACTIONS

TIME MANAGEMENT

THE FIRST TIME I saw this suggestion, I won't say I rolled my eyes, but I didn't exactly make it a burning priority. However, it is from the book I most universally recommend, *Limitless* by Jim Kwik, and therefore it's a practice that deserved a try and subsequently, inclusion in this book.

When scheduling distractions, the first place to look is where you want distractions on your calendar. Or looked at from the opposite lens, where do you want to absolutely avoid distractions? I want to avoid distractions at the library, in my office, at the gym, on the train, or at dinner. These are some of my most productive, full-attention-requiring times on the calendar, so distractions can't go here. So where *can* distractions go on the calendar? Distractions are most welcomed when I'm preparing dinner, especially when it requires long cook times in the oven; at the pool or beach; having lunch; or my personal favorite—driving.

Anyone who wanted to chat earlier in the day, I try to connect with while in the car. Why? Well, if you skipped Practice 64, in short, I can't work while driving, so options are limited. Any conversation someone wants to have that I know could or should go past a couple minutes, I try to ask if it can be done during my next car ride.

Now that you know where you do and don't want to be distracted, next up is when: Are there lulls in your day when the distraction is most welcomed?

For me, that pesky postlunch 3:00 to 4:15 p.m. window is when I'm usually most open to a couple minutes of distraction if I'm not in a meeting. If I have the time available, this is a window when I'll try to get outside for a few steps, get a tea, or sit outside and tend to the items I'd label as distractions— distractions in the sense that they take me away from my work, not in the negative connotation that implies anything less worthy or anything bad.

One thing that erodes flow and consistent output is distraction, whether it's a mental distraction or a literal one—they are both serious. Don't let distraction(s) steal any more of your brain's attention. Put time down on your calendar to address them. Much like the big frog that we'll address in a couple pages, distractions are sure to hold your calendar, and clarity, hostage. ∎

61. DO ONE TASK AT A TIME

TIME MANAGEMENT

ONE OF THE MOST powerful passages in Johann Hari's *Stolen Focus* is his discourse, research, and interviews on multitasking.

Multitasking eats upward of 40 percent of the average worker's day, and the minions of multitasking don't stop there. These carnivorous siphons not only suck up the meatiest parts of our days, but they also drain creativity, diminish memory, increase error rates, and, to top it all off, cause a ten-point drop in IQ. What began as a point of pride we glowingly refer to as "multitasking" ends up being a calendar terror we should injuriously refer to as "multithrashing."

If four detrimental hits to your productivity weren't enough, the inseparable pair of multitasking and switching costs (the effort required to move from one task to another) deliver one more powerful blow: the time of *lost focus*. It takes on average twenty-three minutes and fifteen seconds, that's 23:15, to get back into focus following a distraction.[3] That's the equivalent of just north of two episodes of *SpongeBob SquarePants* or one episode of *Seinfeld*, or in modern-day terms, that's over fifteen consecutive full-length Instagram reels. If we already have so many things to battle, like a distraction every three minutes at work, why make it more difficult to focus? Why increase friction?

Mihaly Csikszentmihalyi wrote about the equivalent of runner's high—the worker's nirvana—when he created the term "flow state" in 1990 in his book of the abbreviated same name: *Flow*. This elevated state where time stops and serenity envelops you into a state beyond consciousness is the apex of output, as studies show flow to result in increases of up to 700 percent in creativity, 500 percent in productivity, and 490 percent in learning rate.[4]

You know the scenes of any superhero movie where they reach some off-the-charts level of power? That's what a flow state is for your brain. It's the holy grail we're seeking yet unknowingly sacrificing each time we try to multitask; reports on the topic show that multitasking and flow states are mutually exclusive.

So monotask, drill, specialize, hyperfocus, or any other way of saying "do *one* task" to do your greatest work. ■

CHECK-IN

Beyond time-stopping and serenity-enveloping, here are a few more ways to confirm you've reached a flow state:

- You don't think of your bodily needs (hunger, thirst, activities of daily living).[5]

- You are so supremely focused that the world around you dissipates or just slips by (e.g., if someone asked you what song was just playing, you wouldn't remember).

- You feel in (complete) control.

- You feel rewarded immediately (just by working on this endeavor!)

60. MINIMIZE DISTRACTIONS

IF YOU LOOK CLOSELY at Robin Sharma's *The 5 AM Club*, you'll realize the title is a bit misleading. The author is not necessarily mandating that you get up at 5:00 a.m. Instead, Sharma is showing us the importance of finding the time when you can exist without distraction by friends, family, or the constant buzz of your phone. For me, this is right about 11:00 p.m., when my wife gets ready for bed and most of the good shows and sporting events are either over or about to wrap up. This time allows me to focus on the quiet and work on what I want to accomplish most—what I feel will contribute the most to my PQO, or prolific quality output.

In addition to not being a morning person—like 8:30-is-early-for-me-to-wake-up kind of nonmorning person—I also find the days when I'm up early to be all about jumping right into my biggest revenue-producing role. To me, early mornings are when you get out ahead of your day, and evenings/nights are up to you to work on your preparation, passion, or position.

I realize this is an opinion, but let me share a little more on this rationale. First off, there's a hard stop to the mornings. When that clock strikes nine, it's time for work at most professional jobs. There is no firm limitation, or cutoff, when it comes to nighttime; you can keep going as long as you like, and while you shouldn't sacrifice sleep, it's easier to justify than being late to work. Secondly, since there is no countdown clock, there is no anxiety about having to get going with your day. With sleep serving as a separator between night and next morning, you have the runway you want to produce, to achieve a flow state, and to not have to worry about the impending 9:00 a.m. alarm bell. While a 5:00 a.m.-to-9:00 a.m. flow state is certainly possible, it's tougher—as the world wakes up, the traffic mounts, and the email inbox proliferates—to remain focused.

While 11:00 p.m. onward has been optimal for my current situation, the moral of the story here is to find what works for you, your chronotype, your environment, and your schedule.

Declutter your mind and environment and at least utilize, if not maximize, this quiet time and golden opportunity. It can be awfully, awfully tempting to just sit in this rare moment of quiet, unwinding with your phone or catching up on TV, but you need to remember that you can do those activities amid the noise and chaos of the world, so why squander this glorious moment?

If you're not feeling particularly inspired or motivated, at least grab a book to feel better about your form of entertainment, productivity, and desired habit formation that's centered on growth and self-improvement. ■

ADDITIONAL TIP

Find ways to minimize stimuli. A great way to do this is to give your desired focal point full view. Whether it's as literal as going full view on your screen, or more interpretative like sitting in the front of the class or reading with your book held upright, do what Stephen Covey recommends and keep the main thing the main thing. When you have the "main thing" taking up the majority, if not 100 percent, of your view, you are mitigating potential issues. In short: Don't give your mind an opportunity to stray.[6]

59. UTILIZE THE TWO-MINUTE RULE

HABIT FORMATION

IN A WORLD of endless entertainment, constant distractions, and an ever-present focus on experiences, it's hard to get started. Oftentimes that's the hardest part. That's why you should utilize the two-minute rule.

If you do a quick Google search you'll see a variety of two-minute rules, including the David Allen two-minute rule that states if something is going to take less than two minutes to complete, do it right away. This "do it now" recommendation has been extended to five minutes or less in this book, so the two-minute rule here is talking about James Clear's two-minute rule as popularized in *Atomic Habits*: If it's a new habit, it should be something you can do in under two minutes.

Whatever task you have a hard time accomplishing or line item you can't seem to cross off your list—do the first two minutes of that activity. Going for a run becomes putting on my running shoes. Reading that new book becomes reading a page of that new book. This principle is tied to making a habit easy and approachable, and it's a nice starting point for kicking off another practice: deconstructing your goals into many smaller subgoals, which we will cover shortly.

To me, this two-minute rule practice is the actualization, the potential to kinetic transition, of the ancient Chinese proverb that says, "The journey of a thousand miles begins with a single step." Find ways to make the journey a crawl, walk, run progression, or more apt for this section: a step, walk, run journey. ■

58. RETIRE AT THE SECOND SIGN OF FATIGUE

TIME MANAGEMENT

WHEN YOU GO TO SLEEP when you're tired, you accomplish a lot. It sounds strange, but it's an easy decision with a powerful downstream impact. You lessen blue light exposure and the effects of catching, or artificially creating, a second wind. You maximize your productivity because you'll be waking up refreshed, ready and able to accomplish great things. You get better sleep, which helps repair your body from the day. Therefore, it's not only a time management boost, but it's also an energy cultivation boost! Going to sleep when you know your body is tired is not only a better utilization of time, it's also an action that will directly lead to greater stores of energy and effectiveness. Look at you being productive by sleeping!

Now the title of this practice isn't to retire at the *first* sign of fatigue for many reasons, and that's because oftentimes at the first sign, you're not actually ready to wind down for bed but rather you're in a lull, you're bored, dehydrated, tired of a particular task, or just plain sad. To make sure you're turning in for the night at the right moment, ask yourself the following:

- *Am I tired or do I need to be rewired?*
  Looking at your step count, time spent outside, and water intake will help you determine if this perceived tiredness is true or if it's a lie masquerading as exhaustion. If you quickly find an energy surge after walking outside and/or having a glass of water, then you know it was a rewiring that was needed.

- *Am I tired or just uninspired?*
  Have you been working on something very repetitive, mentally taxing, or that you just hate to do? Being tired or sacked by a task might mean switching tasks instead of retiring for the evening.

- *Do I need a break or bed?*
  What is a little trickier to determine is the length of rest time needed. Perhaps you've been on your feet for a long time or sustaining an activity for a long period of time and simply sitting down would help. This varies person to person, but if my mind keeps working rapidly

without anxiety, and I can't sit in one precise position for longer than two minutes, then I need a break.

· *Do I stand to gain more by an early night or catching a second wind?*
As this gamut of questions continues, this one is perhaps the one that's most often overlooked. Frankly, this question deserves its own decision-making tree. However, given that you're likely very tired when considering this question, a quick mental pro/con list is more suitable. Begin this pro/con process by asking yourself:
  · Is getting up earlier and working the next day more feasible than catching a second wind tonight?
  · How long of a second wind do I usually catch, and is going to bed at (current time plus second-wind time) reasonable?
  · Would the second wind do more harm than good?

In other words, this exercise is to help you determine: *Do I maximize the moment or mitigate the risk?* ∎

57. EAT THE BIGGEST FROG FIRST

THIS CONCEPT, equally attributed to both Mark Twain and Brian Tracy, paints a rather daunting picture if we stop and really think about it. For those of us who don't eat frogs, I'm going to paint an even more unappetizing picture.

The frog, which you already do not find appetizing, continues to grow each time you put off eating it. You're being forced to eat it with no way out, and its size only continues to grow and grow…and grow, until both the thought and the task of eating the frog are all-consuming. Now with that anxiety-producing backdrop, let's continue.

If scheduling your distraction or task isn't enough—eat it. And eat it now. The lost clarity and lost productivity you'll endure by putting off the daunting task will come at the expense of your good habits and other implemented maximizers.

Not only can it sink your productivity, but if—God forbid—it's pushed out past the day, it can ruin your sleep as well. In which case, not only is it jeopardizing your day, but it's also making you go stir crazy at night. This in turn has an impact on your sleep quality and quantity, which—you guessed it—makes you less productive the next day as well.

You may go to bed thinking you're fine, but 3:30 a.m., pitch-black, anxiety-induced "you" doesn't understand; no matter how rational you try to be in your argument against yourself, panic has taken the reins.

The more you can reduce the time spent on an anxiety-inducing task, the more you can reduce the size of said task, the power it holds over you, and the time spent on its prolonged presence. In addition to shrinking this worrisome task down to size, you produce more overall, as you're no longer lost in the downward spiral of your rumination. ■

56. RESPECT THAT BUILDING A HABIT TAKES TIME

IF YOU'RE FAMILIAR with habit formation at all, chances are you've heard the old adage that it takes twenty-one days to form a new habit and ninety days to build a new way of life. But is this really true? What actually is the amount of time it takes to build a new habit?

The most widely accepted answer comes from a study done by the European Journal of Social Psychology, and it tells us that the time it takes to develop a new habit varies greatly—from 18 to 254 days, in fact.[7] The average from this study came out to 66 days, or about two months and four days. So a July 1 start means the average new habit would be formed, as measured by its achievement of automaticity (or doing something automatically), by September 5.

The study went on to say that missing once did not significantly alter results for timetables—good news for those of us who have very variable days. But as James Clear says, "Missing once is an accident, but missing twice is the start of a new habit," so do what you can to get back up on that hypothetical horse the next day.[8]

To make a strange but hopefully memorable analogy—think of yourself as a caterpillar. A caterpillar cannot transform into a butterfly in one stage, and its progression is not overnight. In fact it takes four stages—egg, caterpillar, chrysalis, and adult—to become a butterfly. To master a habit, you must battle through stages as well. What makes this analogy even more interesting: The time to adulthood from caterpillar ranges from 34 to 207 days, much akin to our 18-to-254-days-habit-formation timeline. Painted lady butterflies reach adulthood in 34 days, while monarch butterflies achieve adulthood in 207 days. So if you're struggling to transform as quickly as you'd like, just realize that perhaps you're not a painted lady or even a zebra longwing, but rather you're the most highly evolved migratory butterfly of all—the rare monarch.

However, unlike a caterpillar, you have the option to take days off and delay or—worse yet—miss your transformation. Stay the course! As Lan Phan writes in her book *Do This Daily*, "Consistency has always been the prerequisite for transformation."[9] It's true in caterpillars and it's true in us. ∎

BE PATIENT.　　　IT'LL BE WORTH IT.

@JUNHANCHIN

55. THEMATICALLY LINK, OR ANCHOR, YOUR HABIT STACKS

THIS FANCY-SOUNDING SKILL is actually quite simple. It effectively gets us to be our own accountability partners, taking advantage of all life's little reminders as opportunities to get more done.

Watering your plant? Grab a glass of water yourself. Telling your friend to take a cold shower for a quick energy boost? Take one yourself. This principle can be rewritten as "practice what you preach, instantly."

This skill, while straightforward, is one I struggled to come up with examples for. So, to not leave you on a cliffhanger, I've compiled ten potential anchors (nine beyond the watering plants example) so that you can *maximize* the application of this skill.

1. Showering? Shower others with encouragement and love (after you finish your shower).
2. Watering the plants? Drink a glass of water yourself.
3. Brushing your teeth? Brush up on your vocabulary or a foreign language.
4. Taking out the trash? Skip the trash TV.
5. Looking in the mirror? Reflect on your mental (or physical) progress.
6. Growing a new item in your garden? Grow a new skill.
7. Exercising your body? Exercise your mind by reading a book (*Dodgeball* movie buffs already know this one).
8. Checking your watch? Have someone watch you check off your to-do list.
9. Cleaning up your home? Clean up your desk, email inbox, or phone notification settings.
10. Turning off the lights at night? Turn off your phone (or at least turn it on airplane mode). ■

54. PRIME YOUR ENVIRONMENT

HABIT FORMATION

FOR THIS SECTION let's place ourselves in our homes. We will cover offices, libraries, cafés, and other potentially optimal locations in other sections but, for now, let's tackle the place where we consistently spend the most time. What can you do to ensure your environment is optimized or, as the title suggests, primed?

Victoria Song in her book *Bending Reality* has a wonderful listing of energizing activities, but there's one in particular I found fascinatingly peculiar, so much so that I added it as one of the guided breaks in the Commence college-to-career training program I co-founded. Titled Designing Your Supercharged Home, it reads: "If your home were to run solely on some kind of energy source that only worked off of positivity and what's good for you, and conversely slowed down or came to a halt if you fed it bad things too, what would you add, subtract, and keep in your home?"[10]

This activity is a wonderful prelude to this section. Now that we have what we need in the home thanks to Victoria, let's set up a system to maximize it.

Let's say your goal is to read a book that's currently getting dusty on your shelf. The first step would be getting it off the shelf and asking where you are most likely to get some reading done.

Answer: in bed before sleep. Clear off your nightstand to have minimal clutter and few potential distractions. If anything, have items that can only serve as *enablers*, like a pen or two, a bookmark, a journal, or a notepad.

Second, ask yourself how you can ensure the space remains dedicated to reading.

Now that your space is cleared, primed, and enabled, avoid cluttering it. What do you usually put on that nightstand? Tea, coffee, water, receipts, change, wallet, phone, keys—and a new place for all of that stuff. A separate end table or entryway table may do the trick.

Third, how can you keep the cue visible?

If you're treating your room as a place only for before, during, and after sleep, then you're not likely to spend much time in your room. Where would your book benefit from being during the day? Perhaps it's that entryway table where you can easily grab it on your way out for a walk, a trip to a park, a doctor's appointment, or anywhere else where you can easily get some light reading done.

There are plenty more things you can do around priming your environment, but if you follow these core three steps, you're sure to accomplish your task in far less time than if the book was merely *around*. In other words, **find ways to turn something from merely *being present* to *having presence*.** ◾

53. MAKE POSITIVITY YOUR DEFAULT

SO MANY OF US look at happiness, fulfillment, and overall satisfaction on an *opt-in* basis: *I'll opt in once I get good news. I'll opt in to feeling fulfilled once that deal comes back. I'll opt in to feeling happy once I get that job. Until then, I'll be disappointed.* Or, to paraphrase the popular *Pawn Stars* meme: Best I can do is blasé. We wear our indifference, toughness, and frosty layer as a badge of honor of sorts. So instead of choosing happiness as an opt-in that occurs when the stars align for a brief moment, how about approaching happiness on an opt-out basis?

What if we open each day expecting that great things are going to transpire, and then we go try and manifest them? I changed my mindset to this a few weeks ago, and it really makes a difference. It's not easy, and there will be many days when you won't even want to try this approach, but what do you have to lose? I am someone who struggles with opting into happiness. I often view it as people being fake, unrealistic, or otherwise unintelligently naive about life. For those who hold similar beliefs, let's address, and subsequently dispatch, each of these three:

1. *Being fake is just pretending everything is fine.* Being fake is when you put on the happy face and pretend everything is fine. If you're genuinely happy, there's no need to put on a happy face, because it's already there. Trying to be happy while being authentic, open, and vulnerable enough to share where you might be struggling or why you're focused more on this attempt at positivity is not only real, it's inspiring. The long and short of it: Perceived phoniness only comes from the combination of putting on the happy face and pretending, or lying to others, that you're happy. If you're honest about what you're trying to do—hats off to you!

2. *Expecting the best is unrealistic and sets you up for disappointment.* This is a tougher mindset to battle, but what's worth calling out is that you can control the expectations you're setting. If you're expecting every day to yield you a million-dollar deal and you're disappointed each day it doesn't happen, you'll likely fail in achieving this "happiness-first" default. However, if you celebrate the little moments—like

beautiful sunsets, happy dogs, a favorite song on the radio—you're more likely to enjoy each day. And akin to those who put on fake smiles and pretend everything is great, don't be someone who denies a bad day when it happens. If the majority of your day (and its four parts) hasn't gone well—that's OK. Acknowledge it and realize that a tough today doesn't deny the potential of a good tomorrow. If you flipped a coin twenty-one times and all twenty-one times it came up tails, what are your odds it'll come up heads the next flip? Still 50 percent. No matter how long you're in a rut, a good day could be tomorrow. Harness that power while setting realistic expectations and approach each conversation like it's going to go well. Eckhart Tolle provides perhaps the most tangible antidote to negativity when he writes in The Power of Now: "A victim identity is the belief that the past is more powerful than the present."[11] If you can truly keep yourself centered on making the best of every now, this mindset will show in your posture, vocal inflection, and smile, and it will naturally invite the other person into a positive discussion.

3. *Those who wake up thinking each day will be great are (nauseatingly) naive.* Maybe you're right. But how often does the always-positive person limit their opportunities by having this rosier-than-thou attitude? Well, assuming this person has the emotional awareness to not be smiling wide at a funeral, I'd say 90 percent-plus of the time being positive serves as a benefit to them. Conversely, those who are afraid to opt in to happiness, and therefore remain apathetic or negative, are limiting themselves 90 percent-plus of the time. I'm not saying you're shutting yourself out completely, but being negative, indifferent, or otherwise diminishing to yourself and others for the sake of trying to say, "I told you so," limits your potential.

If you're like me and you sometimes find yourself reveling in the I told you so's, adopt a different expression. Instead of endeavoring to say, "I told you so," look to prove "I knew we could." After all, no pessimist ever changed the world for the better. ■

Write down your best days and keep a log of them. You'll soon realize great days can happen any day of the week, any week of the month, any month of the year. Endeavor to have a "podium" day each day you wake up. Make it a gold, silver, or bronze September 7, October 9, April 18, November 21, or whatever other day strikes you as random.

WHY WORRY ABOUT A HALF EMPTY CUP...

...WHEN YOU HAVE SO MANY MORE OPTIONS?

52. BE (BRUTALLY) TRANSPARENT WITH YOURSELF

AS A SOCIETY we tend to make excuses, and we tend to view our actions as more productive, more valuable, or more intensive than they really are or were. This is an easy one to fall prey to but also one with an equally simple solution: Hold yourself to your own standards—not the standards of others or your interpretation of their standards.

Ask yourself, would you open the email you just sent out? Would you like that post you uploaded? Would you follow your own account? The point of this exercise isn't to be relentlessly difficult on yourself, as we've seen how poorly that can go for perfectionists, but rather to do something as simple as proofreading or double-checking your work with this new lens. So instead of hitting send because it's already taken too much time, do a quick review and see a way or two it could be improved. Make it response-worthy. Make it something you're proud of.

All this is to say, are you:

1. keeping an accurate score or giving yourself the benefit of the doubt?
2. overlooking some shortcomings and letting things slide?

To put it another way: Is your identity as rock solid as you think?

You can test this by assessing: How often are you guilty of the inverse of your desired, or subscribed, identity?

Brené Brown in her book *Daring Greatly* has an excellent section on this. She writes, "The space between our practiced values (what we're actually doing, thinking, and feeling) and our aspirational values (what we want to do, think, and feel) is the value gap, or what I call 'the disengagement divide.'"[12]

Brown goes on to give examples that include aspirational values of honesty and integrity, and practiced values of rationalizing and letting things slide. The cashier who doesn't scan the sodas at the bottom of the cart is the provided example. Do you go back in and pay for the sodas? Or do you drive off rationalizing how they missed it, it's their fault, they don't need the money anyhow, and/or it'd be such an inconvenience to walk back inside?

While some of you may be reading along thinking, *Well, this doesn't make someone a dishonest person,* this is just one of those, depending upon your perspective, acceptable exceptions or "gray areas."

This shows we tend to view things as binary up front—we're either honest or we're dishonest—and situational in hindsight—it depends on, that's not too bad, etc. While situations can be varied, we still believe identity is binary, and we just selectively round to whatever we feel is more true. We think that since we're more often than not people of integrity it means we are integrous, whereas in actuality we might be 80 percent integrous. And the converse side of integrous is dishonest or untrustworthy, and no one wants to label themself as such, and for good reason—we don't need another negative label dragging us down.

So what should you do? As Lan Phan puts it in her book *Do This Daily,* "The key is maintaining a beginner's mindset throughout your life; that's where the true victory lies."[13] With a beginner's mindset, you are continuously seeking to improve. This will help you continue to push further, do better, and refine your identity label so that you always earn it in your mind. Don't view the label, whether self-appointed or societally recognized, as an opportunity to stop. In fact, with a beginner's mindset you will keep yourself from viewing performance as the measuring stick, using potential and progression as the markers of success. ■

51. FIND, MAXIMIZE, AND RECALL AWE-INSPIRING MOMENTS

MOTIVATION AND ALIGNMENT

IF I ASKED YOU right now to describe a moment that took your breath away, I bet you would have a vivid mental picture in your mind at the ready. These moments not only live with instant accessibility in our memories but also serve to inspire us to accomplish more and to open new creative gateways. The power of awe and wonder shows us what the world is capable of and serves as a great motivator to call upon time and again. This power of awe is increasingly important as we become a society more and more focused on experiences.

During my 2023 visit to Las Vegas, awe-inspiring moments came to rescue me from a time of personal *weltschmerz* (near translation is world-weariness, world pain) and pessimism about the lack of people seeking to better themselves. I had come in feeling low that many societal factors of technology, world leadership, scapegoating, escaping, and ghosting had amalgamated into an unstoppable force, whose by-product was a blasé relinquishing of accountability and acceptance of languor.

In simpler terms, I was observing and battling a "nothing matters, nobody cares, so why bother trying" mindset.

This depressing mindset changed when watching *The Ultimate Variety Show* in Vegas. There was a series of impossible-for-the-average-person feats being performed with precision. There was a man who could balance himself on top of nearly a dozen differently shaped and sized boards; a woman who could pull herself up, invert, and level out horizontally using just one arm; a man who could simultaneously use more than twenty Hula-Hoops; and many more mind-boggling feats. It got me thinking, if there are people right in front of my eyes who can do the seemingly impossible, then there're even more people who can do and do well, who can seek out greatness in themselves and others.

Vince Lombardi, widely considered one of the greatest football coaches of all time, is famous for saying, "The quality of a person's life is in direct proportion to their commitment to excellence." So, inspired and instilled by these elite performers, the question is: Where can you make a full commitment to excellence in your life? ∎

SECTION CHECK-IN

My Three to Five Potential Practices:

1. _____

   _____

2. _____

   _____

3. _____

   _____

4. _____

   _____

5. _____

   _____

50. FIND FLOW THROUGH MUSIC

MOTIVATION AND ALIGNMENT

ONE OF THE MOST difficult things is finding a way to break away from others. Whether it be a break in conversation, text, games, or DMs, it just seems that breaking away before you've expended every ounce of energy is considered rude. And if you do somehow find a magical way to break free, the opportunity peters out, as you can't seem to summon the energy to be productive. Or let's say you do manage to have the energy, you find some quiet space, but what you don't have is the focus to make the most of your time, and then before you know it—*poof*—another golden opportunity slips through your fingertips. Gone. So what can you do to capitalize on the opportunity and quickly and effectively tap into focus?

In *Limitless*, Jim Kwik tells us about the power of baroque music. Kwik cites learning expert Chris Boyd Brewer when he shares, "Baroque music… creates an atmosphere of focus that leads students into deep concentration in the alpha brain wave state."[1]

That's helpful; however, I don't know about you, but I'm *not* feeling 1722. At least not very often. So what else can you do to use music to harness the power of concentration and, cue Eminem, "lose yourself" in the music?

A no-words playlist that can include songs like "Fortune Days" by the Glitch Mob, "Mammoth" by Dimitri Vegas, "Cleaning Apartment" by Clint Mansell, and "Into the Wild" by Nora En Pure is sure to have you producing some of your most focused, inspired work.

For more songs to choose from for finding your flow, here are ten of my favorite songs from four of my most productive playlists:

Repetitive Rhythms for Focused Flow

1. "50000 Watts of Funkin" by Edgar Uroz
2. "The Rockafeller Skank" by Fatboy Slim
3. "Slow Ride" by Foghat
4. "Million Voices" by Otto Knows
5. "Allein" by Pryda
6. "Music Sounds Better with You" by Stardust
7. "Out of Touch" by Uniting Nations

8. "C O O L" by Le Youth
9. "The Bomb!" by the Bucketheads
10. "2 Legit 2 Quit" by MC Hammer

No Distractions

1. "Top Gun Anthem" by Lorne Balfe
2. "Aggressive Expansion" by Hans Zimmer
3. "Fortune Days" by the Glitch Mob
4. "Intro" by the xx
5. "Cream on Chrome" by Ratatat
6. "Into the Wild" by Nora En Pure (which to me sounds like they're saying "here come the best")
7. "Moon" by Kid Francescoli
8. "New Orleans" by Naxxos
9. "Waikiki" by Deep Chills
10. "No Man No Cry" by Jimmy Sax

These ten are a good start for an open-to-close playlist, but if you're looking to spice up the middle of this set with something more dramatic, "Bond on Bond" by BOND, "Battle Without Honor or Humanity" by Tomoyasu Hotei, and "Kashmir" by Escala could be some valuable options.

You Got This

1. "Fire" by Barns Courtney
2. "Thunder" by Imagine Dragons
3. "How You Like Me Now?" by the Heavy
4. "Thunderstruck" by AC/DC
5. "I Want to Take You Higher" by Sly & the Family Stone
6. "Change" by Kodi Lee
7. "Till I Collapse" by Eminem
8. "Tubthumping" by Chumbawamba
9. "Giant" by Calvin Harris
10. "Titanium" by David Guetta

Pump Up:

1. "Bring the Noise" by Anthrax
2. "Guerrilla Radio" by Rage Against the Machine
3. "Beast" by Thomas Gold
4. "Shoot to Thrill" by AC/DC
5. "Immigrant Song" by Led Zeppelin
6. "I Can't Stop" by Flux Pavilion
7. "The Hum" by Dimitri Vegas
8. "Can't Hold Us" by Macklemore
9. "Stop the Rock" by Apollo 440
10. "Booyah" by Showtek ◼

49. EXERCISE SOMETIME BEFORE 7:00 P.M., AROUND ONE TO TWO HOURS BEFORE YOU NEED TO BE YOUR SHARPEST

ENERGY CULTIVATION

NOT ALL HOURS are created equal. The finalist meetings, presentations, speeches—they all have a disproportionate impact on our financial, professional, and social well-being. Some items are the culmination of our week's, month's, year's—DECADE's—hard work and research jammed into one (twenty-minute) presentation. Nervous? Well, we've got something for that. Feeling drained at the very thought of this scenario? Got something for that too. It's the same remedy for both: exercise.

Why exercise? Well, for starters, it's a heck of a lot more beneficial than coffee, and lucky for you, it's something that so few people prioritize doing (at the optimal time), making it an extra differentiator for you over everyone else. Think of yourself as an elite athlete preparing for your big event. Elite athletes spend their day preparing to be at their peak at the right time. It's why they have specific game-day rituals and preparation like warm-ups, stretching, etc. This way, when the moment comes, they can't blame lack of physical preparation or time management for their performance. However, this is not the case when it comes to many (elite) professionals. If their big meeting is later in the day, the meeting constituents are getting whatever energy is left by that time. Even many of the most gifted presenters, persuaders, negotiators, and analysts miss their opportunity for peak performance simply because of societal constructs that make it cripplingly uncomfortable to step away and revitalize.

While some give their WLO or "what's left over" energy, and others seek their low-effort fixes like coffee or an energy drink, you're offered a massive competitive edge. No matter how superior a competitor, if they're not primed for performance, fresh, and focused, they'll lose their advantage, as a quick fix cannot compete with the benefits of exercise.

For this reason, you can think of exercise as a cup of super coffee: It makes you more alert, without the negative side effects, and helps improve your mood as well. Am I biased? Well, considering I don't drink coffee and am writing this passage from the treadmill, maybe. So let's look at the science instead.

In a study by Western University in Ontario, they tested coffee consumption versus exercise. They determined that just twenty minutes of exercise showed very similar cognitive benefits to that of a cup of coffee. Not bad, considering it takes about just as long to walk or drive to your nearest coffee shop, order, and begin drinking the cup. It becomes even better when you consider there's a much lower risk of crashing from exercise than coffee, and according to Harvard Health, a short burst of exercise increases mental acuity as much as or even more than coffee and for a longer period of time. It becomes no contest when you consider exercise comes without coffee's potential side effects like insomnia, anxiety, increased heart rate, or headaches, and without the increased risk of high cholesterol, bone loss, and arthritis.[2]

The National Library of Medicine found that feelings like decreased negative affect, increased positive affect, and decreased stress have been reported to last up to twenty-four hours past exercise cessation, and improvements in attention, working memory, verbal fluency, and decision-making have shown demonstrable improvement for up to two hours after exercise.[3]

In short, the science shows us that you'll do yourself a world of good if next time you have a big presentation scheduled, you block off your calendar for exercise beforehand. ■

48. USE PERFORMANCE ENHANCERS

ENERGY CULTIVATION

THE PHRASE *performance enhancers* has a negative, borderline illegal, connotation. I'm sure many of you have conjured up images of the 1994–2004 steroid era of baseball or thought of phrases like doping, steroids, cheating, etc.

Performance enhancers don't have to be illegal, especially not when it comes to productivity and the mind.

Dr. Daniel Amen, a noted brain scientist, talks about how the "prettiest" brains he's studied take ginkgo biloba to improve memory and blood flow to the brain. Why is this important?

According to a study published in *Psychology Today*, blood flow to the brain can significantly increase neurocognitive functioning, verbal fluency, and executive functions like memory, inhibition, and problem-solving.[4]

Conversely, Dr. Amen shares that reduced blood flow is the number one brain scan predictor that a person will develop Alzheimer's.[5] When we think of productivity, we should not only think about the immediate and short term, but also our long term. When it comes to our health, it's not just about adding years to our life, but also life to our years. You can begin safeguarding your brain health and blood flow with ginkgo biloba, multivitamins, vitamin D, magnesium, and every item listed in Practice 47.

Rhodolia, a popular supplement in Chinese medicine, is said to help reduce fatigue or tiredness, but more research is required. The same goes for resveratrol.[6] SAMe has been shown to help those with depression, acetyl-L-carnitine can help those suffering from a loss of brain function, while bacopa monnieri is effective when taken daily for several weeks. Lastly, fish oil supplements, some of the most popular, are most beneficial for those who cannot get two servings of oily fish per week.

For those of you seeking supplements to boost your physical performance, which in turn will help propel you forward mentally, the National Institutes of Health published a helpful chart of all supplements, foods, and compounds recommended to improve performance, alongside their potential side effects and cross-referenced studies to highlight true potential benefit.[7] ■

47. EAT ANTIOXIDANT-LADEN AND NUTRIENT-RICH FOODS

ENERGY CULTIVATION

WHILE NOT THE most original topic, it's an important one. And despite all the clamor, can anyone really rattle off the definitive list of best foods for your brain health?

I was tired of seeing a laundry list of foods to eat. It felt like anything outside of Skittles and Twinkies was using the magic three-word, approval-seeking phrase: "Great source of."

So I decided to do my own research and tabulate the best of the best, top of the top, crème de la crème of brain-boosting foods.

I pulled the top ten most reputable sources on best brain foods and cross-examined them to find eight clear winners: four standouts that appeared on almost every list and four that appeared on the majority. The four superstars were walnuts, blueberries, salmon, and green leafy vegetables.

Walnuts swept across all categories for perhaps the most varied of benefits, beginning with high omega-3 fatty acids for faster information processing and overall brain health and memory. Walnuts also contain polyphenols and antioxidants to promote brain health and stave off mental decline. They are nutrient rich and help bone, skin, and gut health. As if not already enough, research showed yet another benefit: Walnuts are a natural source of melatonin, helping you regulate sleep. Basically, if you're not allergic to nuts, you should try and get into these.

Salmon (and other fatty fish such as sardines and tuna) was a prominent inclusion for its high concentration of omega-3 fatty acids. Many may know the benefits of omega-3s (especially since we just covered it), so I'm moving on to a far-less-often-discussed, near namesake: omega-6. Dr. Romie Mushtaq tells us about the importance of balancing omega-3 and omega-6 on a 1:1 basis in her book *The Busy Brain Cure*. Contrary to omega-3 being jam-packed in fatty fish, omega-6 is most densely found in vegetable oils and in seeds like pumpkin or sunflower.[8] Of course it can also be found in the omnipresent superfood: walnuts!

Blueberries, as a rich source of antioxidants, anthocyanins, and folate, made almost all lists. The antioxidants help prevent decline while folate helps neurotransmitters function.

Green leafy vegetables were great for folate and antioxidants like the above-mentioned blueberries, but also for beta-carotene, which research shows may boost memory; lutein, which has been shown to help cognitive abilities (especially among those advanced in age); and vitamin K, which (similar to lutein) shows benefits for older adults and the elderly. In fact, one study from a university medical center in Chicago found that those who regularly ate 1.3 daily servings of green leafy vegetables showed cognitive abilities of those eleven years their junior, showing us that age is just a number...if you eat your leafy greens.[9]

The next four most frequently cited super foods were dark chocolate, tea/coffee, eggs, and whole grains.

Dark chocolate, like its predecessors, has powerful antioxidants. One antioxidant that is unique to dark chocolate is flavanols, which are essential for the growth and survival of brain cells. Perhaps less surprisingly, dark chocolate can help blood flow, increase mood, and—a little less obvious benefit—it can also help protect against age-related memory loss. Before fellow chocolate lovers rejoice, it's worth noting that much of the studies and benefits are linked to dark chocolate with 70 percent cacao and higher. So next time you reach for a chocolate bar at the grocery store, endeavor to up your cacao percentage.

Next up in the Super 8: tea and coffee. Both (caffeinated) tea and coffee contain antioxidants called flavonoids to reduce brain inflammation. Furthermore, some studies tie caffeine to improved memory and concentration, and reduced risk of dementia, stroke, and Alzheimer's.

While we've discussed some of the downsides of coffee in prior sections, the combination of tea and coffee in moderation seems to be the winning recipe.

If you don't consider yourself a tea drinker, consider this: Research from *Ikigai: The Japanese Secret to a Long and Happy Life* shows white tea could be the natural product with the highest concentration of antioxidants (polyphenols) in the world.[10] One cup of white tea packs the punch of about twelve cups of OJ.

Like coffee, eggs came up on the list with various benefits but also a couple drawbacks—especially around cholesterol, high saturated fat content, and linkages to cancer and diabetes. On the brain-boosting side, eggs had, no surprise here, high antioxidants, especially lutein. Egg yolk's high prevalence of choline also promotes good neural communication between brain cells, aiding in verbal memory, and is an especially helpful benefit for development in children.[11]

Lastly, whole grains appeared on the list more so as a lesser of evils to their alternatives, but with pronounced benefits in folate density, which is particularly impactful, as folate can help memory.

While this scientific section may not be the most enjoyable read, its takeaways are important. For maximal impact, here's a nontechnical, action-packed recap: Eat many (more) walnuts, a balance of salmon/sardines or other fatty fish, and lots of blueberries and green leafy vegetables. Use a moderate approach to key brain boosters like dark chocolate, eggs, tea, and coffee (especially coffee). If you're reaching for bread, go for whole grain. ■

46. STAY HYDRATED

ENERGY CULTIVATION

YOUR BRAIN IS only 2 percent of your mass, but it consumes 20 percent of your energy.[12] It's a demanding little thing, but since it governs you, you need to give it what it wants. Think of the Snickers commercial—never-ending with its negativity and attention-seeking when it's unsatisfied, yet calm, productive, and happy when satiated.

So, just how much water should you consume in a day? Is it the old eight eight-ounce cups a day formula? Or the slightly more complex but just as common recommendation and calculation: half your body weight in ounces per day in water?

The answer is neither.

According to the National Academies of Science, Engineering, and Medicine, it's 91 ounces for women and 125 ounces for men.[13]

Before you panic that you're below this amount, the operative word from this study was *consume*, and we consume water from many sources beyond just filling up our glasses.

When looking further I found a helpful guide complete with a situational chart of glasses of water recommendations depending on your age, gender, and other factors (like exercise and breastfeeding) from Harvard.[14] The most common recommendation for adult men was 104 ounces and for adult women, 72 ounces. Considering that we get about 20 percent of our water from sources outside of actually drinking water, this report and the NASEM study seem to align fairly well.

To maximize H2O retention, minimize nausea, and overall just lead a healthier lifestyle, try to avoid chugging water in short intervals.[15] You should instead keep a steady, throughout-the-day approach to your water intake and be sure to drink water before and during meals to make your hydration most effective.

So, what would steady water intake look like? For a man it's simple, as a liter of water is just under thirty-four ounces and therefore almost exactly a third of the recommended daily amount. So, three liters of water would just about do it. Let's say if you're up for sixteen hours per day and begin your day at 8:00 a.m., this would mean finishing your first liter by 1:20 p.m., your second by 6:40 p.m., and your third by midnight. This could quite simply mean one by lunch, two by dinner, and three by bed. For women, two liters would get you close at about sixty-eight ounces, but for precision, three twenty-four-ounce bottles would do it on the same schedule.

Here are a couple other tips I came across when researching that I thought might be helpful to include:

1. Despite people's preference for drinking cold water, room-temperature water is more likely to be consumed in the necessary quantities.
2. As you age, your thirst declines, so tracking your water intake becomes more important.
3. Just a 2 percent water deficit can introduce symptoms such as mood changes (e.g., irritability), fatigue, confusion, or even memory loss.

45. UNDERPROMISE AND OVERDELIVER

TIME MANAGEMENT

DURING A PODCAST I was on, someone asked me what I considered to be the top skill among sales folks. That answer, as they knew, was featured in my first book, *100 Skills of the Successful Sales Professional*, but what surprised me was their follow-up question: What would you say is the top skill for someone in consulting? Or better yet, how about the top skill for any client-facing position? Given where I'm writing this passage, you may have already guessed the answer: underpromise and overdeliver. This one simple principle has a disproportionate impact on your success, because much of life is about setting expectations.

Now, if you're wondering what in the world this has to do with productivity, it's quite simple. The under/over principle allows you to better prioritize, have greater peace of mind, and complete better work. Not to mention, God forbid someone misses your request or their work is delayed and you do not employ this principle, the pressure and stress of being late on a task will compromise your clarity and productivity—much like the big frog we covered earlier.

To leverage this principle to its fullest: First, find out what timeline is customary for this task. For example, let's say five days is customary, it's readily able to be completed in four, and it can be pressed to finish in three.

Second, indicate to your clients/constituents a range that allows for 20 to 50 percent more time. In this example, communicate a timeline of six to eight days.

Third, communicate your own internal target prior to that timeframe—four days if you're in good keeping with the resources carrying out the task, or the full five days if you're in a neutral or negative position internally with your team.

Fourth, check in on that internal target date to see if things are coming along well. Most of the time you'll be able to proofread and send by day five, a full day ahead of schedule. But in those moments where something is delayed, you're still in the clear. And if somehow, some way, someone completely forgot, you can expedite in three days and still deliver on time.

Fifth and finally, proof your work and send it on time, or 20 percent ahead of schedule. Be careful about your windows, because if you routinely send things well in advance, folks will think you're "sandbagging" your time and will question future timelines. ■

44. FIND YOUR MOST PRODUCTIVE ENVIRONMENTS, SETUPS, AND LOCATIONS

PRODUCTIVE ENVIRONMENTS should be:

1. Clean
2. Distraction-free
3. Non-context-mixed

Most essential is number three: non-context-mixed. In other words, you should avoid mixing the context of how you use a space at all costs. The more you can convince your memory that this is a place of purity, the better off you'll be.

For me, libraries, trains, and planes are my three most sanctified spaces. Everyone knows not to try and derail me off my productivity track—pun intended.

When I do end up having to make plans while I'm still working at the library, I will get up and either go outside or walk to another place in the library. In addition to getting some steps, this relocation ensures that specific seat and table remain "holy" and pure.

If you find yourself deviating from your work, ask yourself: *Do I think I'll remember I did this task here? Do I want to remember that I did this task here?* If the task is any deviation from your productivity—the answer is no.

Two important callouts here: First, *this doesn't mean this spot is only for laborious drudgery.* That's not only unrealistic, but you also risk creating a gateway or pathway to hating this sanctified space. Just the other day I spent my time in one of my pure spaces (a table at the gym) working on booking a happy hour. Looking up bar menus and fun activities isn't exactly the worst thing in the world, but it was for an event that means a lot to one of my business endeavors. So this activity was driving my endeavors forward, and it passed the two questions—I will remember doing this here, and I'm good with remembering it, because it falls neatly in one of the seven areas of my life related to professional productivity.

Another question to ask yourself is: *Is this situation isolatable?* Can you realistically say, "This is totally outside of the norm and therefore will not defile the sanctification of my space"? ∎

A good example is an office party. Two hundred days of the year you're in the office, and outside of the summer office party and winter holiday party, you're heads-down working. That kind of 100:1 ratio is not likely to defile your space. My more frequent example is the train. Weekdays during the day? I need to keep that headspace tight and keep working so I don't fall into a rhythm where my phone is welcomed. But a Friday night at 11:00 p.m. after dinner and drinks with some friends? Different story. It's not the time, the day, or the headspace to interfere with my productivity.

If you have reasonable distinctions—emphasis on distinctions, *plural*— to keep you away from jeopardizing the brain association you have with the space, you'll be OK. Just don't let that 9:00 a.m., Tuesday morning *oh I want to watch the basketball highlights from last night's game* get in the way. This is especially important because there're eighty-two *regular* season games, not to mention the postseason, so this one-off could very easily become a one-hundred-off. I unfortunately fell into a mini rhythm of this issue during some amazing Steph Curry games, and it took me longer than I care to admit to get back on track. As James Clear says, "Missing once is an accident. Missing twice is the start of a new habit."[16] Don't let bad new habits sully the purity of your space. With all of this said, I'm not sacrificing my Steph Curry highlights (did you know this man made 105 straight three-point shots? Statistically, you're more likely to be struck by lightning multiple consecutive times), I'm just making sure that I'm conscientious about where I watch. ■

43. BEGIN CULTIVATING TINY HABITS— THINGS YOU CAN DO IN UNDER A MINUTE

TINY HABITS, an impactful book by renowned behavioral scientist BJ Fogg, is the impetus behind this suggestion. Fogg defines a tiny habit as something that:

1. is easy to do,
2. takes thirty seconds or less, and
3. is a consistent activity you carry out daily.[17]

What I love about this is not only how readily available the opportunities are, but also their intended length. When it's something this short, it gives us a chance to take a break. In this way it's a double benefit—both adherence to positive habit formation and a break.

Tiny habits are things like flossing, brushing your teeth, giving a hug to a loved one—the possibilities are endless. I personally use brushing my teeth, putting in contacts, and giving my wife a shoulder massage when I need to take a minute's break. These tiny habits better your health, mood, and even relationships!

As relationship expert Dr. John Gottman would tell you, it takes only a six-second kiss or a twenty-second hug to release oxytocin. Heck, even a six-second kiss and a twenty-second hug *combined* are under thirty seconds, making this the quickest habit stack I can think of![18]

One thing to be careful of is using the thirty-second break to check something on your phone. Slipping into the bad habit of "filling the void" by mindlessly scrolling on your phone is a vortex that lures you into a bottomless pit, a vacuum where time and memory do not exist.

Distance yourself from this bad habit and others like it so much that you don't even label it a *habit*. Let's replace it with one letter down on the keyboard and call a bad habit a nabit. Nabit—sounds like the shortened form of the minced oath interjection dagnabbit that we might hear from a cartoon character when something goes wrong. Or like the word nab, which is defined as to catch someone doing something wrong. Perfect association. See? Breaking bad habits, or nabits, comes right down to breaking them down linguistically. Instead of wasting thirty seconds on your phone, we can create our own cancel culture in just as much time with changing bad habit to nabit. ■

PRO TIP

Looking for a fourth and perhaps most impactful step to the above tiny habits recipe from Fogg's book? Immediate positive reinforcement. Smile, jump for joy—celebrate the step you've taken. It may sound obscure, childish, or amateurish, but it'll make for a positive association and an action that's more likely to turn into a habit.

42. DECONSTRUCT YOUR GOAL INTO MANY SMALLER, SMART SUBGOALS

AS JIM KWIK likes to say: Inch by inch, life's a cinch. Yard by yard, life is hard.

One expedited way to ensure you won't accomplish anything substantial is to let the sheer size of a goal get in the way. Take what's happening right here—writing a book—as an example. It's perhaps the single thing I've done that elicits the biggest shock. People always ask with great fervor, "How long did it take you??" When I respond with "three months," they seem shocked. When I explain how it was done through SMART goals and through making action the utmost priority, even above quality, the shock value wears away.

When you have SMART (specific, measurable, attainable, realistic, and time-bound) goals, you're on your way, and when you move your mindset from "I need to publish a book" back to "I need to write a single page" or "I need to edit or outline what I want to say," it becomes a lot easier.

Even if people don't know what each letter stands for, the concept of SMART goals is widely known. What's less commonly known is the John Whitmore model. Whitmore expands upon SMART to form SMARTPURECLEAR. PURE is positively stated, understood, relevant, and ethical, while CLEAR is challenging, legal, environmentally sound, agreed, and recorded.

Overall I like this expanded version. SMART is hackneyed and misses a few elements, and despite being slightly verbose, the Whitmore model adds some very necessary components, especially PUREC. While they're all important, some can be implied. Ethical could/should incorporate legal and environmentally sound, while agreed and recorded can be done within realistic and measurable, respectively. But as for the others: You can have SMART goals that aren't challenging or SMART goals that aren't positively stated. Worse yet, you can create a wonderful SMART goal but have no idea what it truly means or translates to from an input perspective. I could tell you right now that I'm going to become a USCF chessmaster within the next twelve years, but I wouldn't really understand that goal nor would I say it's relevant for what I'm looking to accomplish. SMART? Sure. It's specific. It's measured by the USCF (2200 or above rating). It's attainable and realistic, as many others have done it in that timeframe or less, and it's time-bound.

So, to make it a bit more memorable and help you maximize your goals, a revised, combined version of these two acronyms could be:

Being SMART (specific, measurable, attainable, realistic, time-bound) is the CURE (challenging, understood, relevant, ethical) that leads to successfully accomplishing your goals. ■

41. GET OUTSIDE

Before you roll your eyes at this common maxim, ask yourself: *How much time have I spent outside recently?*

There's a good chance the answer is under thirty minutes per day—a 44 percent chance, according to the National Health and Nutrition Examination Survey (NHANES), to be exact.[19]

Your knee-jerk response may be, "Oh, not me! I'm outside often!" but once you do the math, you may realize our propensity to overestimate.

Think about most of your time spent outdoors; what are you doing? My first guess would be commuting. This entails walking to your car, or the train, and subsequently walking from the lot/station to the office. If you're not bringing your lunch too, then you might add some outside time to your day by picking up lunch. Once the day is done, it's the inverse of the morning commute—from the office back to said station, and from the car/station back into your home.

Outside of this time during the workweek, when else do you reliably, consistently spend time outside? From the parking lot into the supermarket is one. The parking lot to the gym is two. Parking lot to the restaurant is a third. And, for a grand display of outdoors: the gas station, where you have… extended parking lot time! If we eliminated parking lot and outdoor commute time, what would we be left with? A whole lot of indoor time. Here's why we need to rethink that:

Of course, there's the well-known vitamin D boost inherent in being outside, but that's far from the only benefit. Studies have shown that ninety minutes of walking in a park is linked to increased neural activity for the part of the brain associated with attention and positive affect.[20] UCLA has found that spending more time outdoors provides both a recharge as well as a boost to the quality of your sleep, which is the ultimate recharge and repair.[21]

Getting outside is often linked to reducing cortisol levels—our body's stress gauge. While you're out there, look up at the sky. I once heard from *Shift the Work* author Joe Mechlinski that it's physically impossible to look up at a blue sky, smile, and jump up and down, and to still feel sad or angry. I always think I look absolutely ridiculous smiling and jumping up and down, which for me produces laughter, and wouldn't you know it—Joe was right. ■

40. THEME YOUR ACTIONS

EARLIER WE SPOKE about thematically linking tasks, where a habit you are already doing can be linked to something else you want to do, like drinking more water by having a cup of water each time you water your plants. In this section, we're scaling this concept to the everyday. While the cues won't be quite as literal, we endeavor to move forward.

Though they may look similar, you wouldn't eat your ice cream and mashed potatoes at the same time, so why would you do this with your work? Theming your actions, and subsequently drilling into one facet, gets you into a rhythm and helps you stay on task. The remaining tasks are clear within that field or facet, and each one you complete builds momentum. Think of pedaling a bicycle: The first few turns of the pedals seem strenuous, but once you're off and biking, it becomes easier. The effort you put in at the beginning has churned the potential energy into kinetic energy, and now—both physically and mentally—you're in a groove.

Theming your actions, or grouping activities in one domain to be completed in succession of one another, not only builds momentum and sustains focus, but it also minimizes switching costs. These switching costs, which we covered in prior practices, are both readily apparent and latent here:

Different types of tasks require different types of thinking, and switching from one type to another can cause undue mental friction. The bigger the difference between two tasks, the greater the amount of mental friction, and more mental friction means a longer adjustment period. In turn, a longer adjustment period requires more time spent strategizing, resulting in higher switching costs. It's a vicious domino cycle, and in a world where you're already combating so many impediments to your focus, you don't need another *trigger*, or catalyst, to unravel into the void. ◼

TRYING TO MULTITASK
GETS YOU NOWHERE

DOING ONE THING AT A
TIME GETS THE JOB DONE

@JUNHANCHIN

39. CREATE A "LOYALTY PROGRAM" FOR YOURSELF

THERE'S AN APP for everything. We all know this, but we don't always know which apps can help us, and worse yet, we don't often engage with the apps that can help us most. Yet one particular app has done an amazing job at building awareness, users, and loyalty: Fetch.

For those who don't know Fetch, in a nutshell it's an app that rewards you for scanning your receipts. Perhaps there was even a deal you didn't know about that you can find on the app before or after you shop. It's a great concept with many loyal users. Will it get you rich? Not that I've seen yet, as a mere twenty-five points—about two cents per scan—is the most likely scan result. Two cents. That's two pennies on the ground. I've seen people yelled at in New York City for giving the needy anything less than a quarter. Yet this penny-giving app has eighteen million users as of late 2023, with more than six million engaging daily. It is valued at over $2.5 billion and employs more than eight hundred people. So how is something that's giving out literal pennies becoming so successful? Simplicity, progress tracking, gamification, and rewards: four things you can find in… your own loyalty program.

The loyalty program, a James Clear recommendation in his book *Atomic Habits*, operates as follows: For each time you forgo an immediate pleasure, contribute to your own long-term fund. This could be for something sizable like a vacation fund, or something more elementary like a night out savings jar. Another way this can work is for every time you accomplish a task, meet a milestone, or hit a larger goal checkpoint, you can reward yourself. Very similar to temptation bundling (covered in detail in Practice 30), a loyalty program for yourself gets you to take action on the difficult tasks and/or sustain focus on the longer-term goals. While temptation bundling may be helpful for the immediate or very near term, this loyalty program gets you chipping away at the long term, seeing the rewards—or in Fetch's case, points—add up. If you can do the following five things in your loyalty program, then you're on your way to accomplishing great things:

1. Make each checkpoint for a *reasonable amount of time* (two to seven days).

2. Make each checkpoint *realistic and progressively increase the difficulty* of checkpoints at every 20 percent interval of the total (think of video game leveling; oftentimes the jump from Level 3 to Level 4 isn't the same as Level 29 to Level 30).

3. Find ways to *give yourself bonus opportunities* for when you inevitably get stuck or less motivated by the everyday checkpoints. Moreover, be sure to find many ways to accumulate points. One of the reasons I believe airlines and hotel chains have struggled with loyalty programs while folks like Fetch are thriving with their rewards program is that Fetch is a catchall—any receipt, any purchase. Airlines and hotels are the opposite—rewarding certain classes of tickets with blackout dates, partnership gaps, etc.

4. *Don't let your streaks run out.* Whether it's a bonus for the streak length or a penalty/deduction for when you break a streak, do whatever you can to keep the loyalty program advancing.

5. The rewards system is *prominently displayed and continuously updated.* If you don't know what the points translate to, don't see it often and easily, and don't see its continuous progression, then it's at risk of failing.

With all these ways to incentivize action, you'll be getting more done on both the work-hard and play-hard fronts, getting to do more while elevating your position in life. For a play on an old Southwest Airlines tagline: You are now free to move about the country('s elite). ∎

38. USE NARROW TIME WINDOW BLOCKS

"Ignoring the facts for short-term gain will almost always bring long-term pain."
—ELDON HENSON

ONE OF THE most subtle, yet substantial, drains on productivity is the half-hour calendar block. It's so prevalent in society that virtually no one fights back against it. It's become the overwhelming default despite it being a simple thing to change.

What makes matters worse is the fact that even when you do book a meeting for, say, fifteen minutes, your calendar still looks like it's booked for half an hour. If it's going to look the same, why fight it? Why not just spend more time talking about nonsense or complaining about the very work you're setting out to do? While the extra time can sometimes be valuable to build more rapport and bond with others, here are four challenges it presents for most scenarios:

1. People end up being late to the meeting, creating friction before they even arrive.
2. It introduces extra time that's often spent complaining, which in and of itself is a drain.
3. It gives you an artificial, or at least inflated, sense of productivity.
4. It lulls you into moving slower throughout the day.

Now, if I really haven't convinced you to move off the thirty-minute default for meetings, we can table that for the time being. But, perhaps more importantly, what about your own calendar time blocks?

Blocking out big chunks of time not only allows us to experience an artificial dopamine spike from calendaring and checking things off our to-do list, but it also risks Parkinson's law, the concept that work expands to fill the time given to complete it.

Ideally you'll now use narrower time blocks for *both* meetings and work blocks, but I'd suggest you highly consider at least one of these two to improve upon in your day-to-day. After all, it's Practice 38 for a reason, and that reason is this practice does something rare: It finds you extra time, time to make your contribution to society and leave your lasting legacy. ■

37. DO YOUR BEST TO MINIMIZE COGNITIVE DISSONANCE

MOTIVATION AND ALIGNMENT

"The more at peace we are, the more productive we can be."
—RYAN HOLIDAY

AS SOMEONE WHO works multiple jobs, has a number of passion projects, and still tries to maintain strong friendships and family relationships, this is perhaps the toughest practice to master.

There are many definitions of cognitive dissonance that all share in common the difficulty or burden one carries by holding competing thoughts at the same time. My favorite definition of cognitive dissonance comes from the Cleveland Clinic: "…that mental space of discomfort, angst, guilt or shame associated with the decisions you're making or the beliefs you're questioning."[22]

The weight of doing one thing while you know, or think, you should be doing another is a large burden to carry, and it can leave you constantly wanting more out of life, in a state of stress, or anxious about when you'll be able to get back to your favorite and/or most lucrative task. However you look at it, cognitive dissonance is a fast track toward the ultimate productivity killer: depression.

Oftentimes this noise is loudest when you're busy with your day job and/or behind on your most reliable work—the work that pays the bills and, hopefully, provides the benefits.

Conversely, and more helpfully, the noise is the lowest on…holidays!

Now you may be saying, "Yeah, right—I'm not going to sacrifice my key family time and religious celebrations." I understand that, and as someone who tries very hard to keep a Sabbath twenty-four hours from 6:00 p.m. Saturday to 6:00 p.m. Sunday, I subscribe to those same values and ideals, but here's the kicker: Most holidays are a two-to-six-hour celebration, leaving you with ten to fourteen other hours to work toward your PQO (prolific quality output). While holidays like Christmas might be on the fuller side of the observation or celebration time commitment, holidays like MLK Day and Memorial Day (which happens to be when I'm writing this passage) are lighter on the time commitment, leaving you plenty of time to work on what you want most. So, for the purpose of this section, let's take a holiday right in the middle of the time commitment spectrum: Thanksgiving.

Thanksgiving, for most folks I know, is an extra day of football. Sure, it might also be an opportunity to catch the parade and is almost always a feast among family and friends, but it's rarely a full workday's worth of activities. For the occasional times it does take the entire day, don't fret. Understand that these days aren't guarantees to get out ahead but rather potential bonus opportunities. If the day presents itself, you carpe diem. If it doesn't, you just enjoy it and hopefully rejuvenate to protect against burnout.

The particular beauty of Thanksgiving is that, for most, it comes with a built-in extra day primed to be a productive day: Black Friday. With about 69 percent of state, local, and government workers getting the day off, and 40 percent of US states recognizing it as a state holiday, a good chunk of the country has an even richer bonus day opportunity.[23]

This Thanksgiving Hangover day is a godsend, because it really doesn't require any time commitments at all. Shopping isn't a religious celebration, and for many it's not even a time commitment at all anymore as shopping is done primarily online for about 37 percent of Americans.[24]

So, while Black Friday is often the throwaway, extra-vacation, long-weekend day, it doesn't have to be.

Not only is the noise the lowest, but the dopamine rush can be the highest. Producing and contributing toward your PQO when no one is expecting anything of you—well, it makes me feel like a superstar, and it can do the same for you. These bonus days, since virtually no one else is being productive, are your opportunities to shine.

You have enough triggers, distractions, and noise to block out; you don't need to battle noise in the six inches between your ears as well. Maximize these low-noise, golden opportunities. ■

36. WORK ON THINGS YOU TRULY LOVE

MOTIVATION AND ALIGNMENT

I KNOW, I KNOW: Boring, overused advice—*Why am I reading a book that gives me the most generic advice at productivity Practice 36?*

~~There's a lot more than meets the eye here~~—If I asked you what you love, would you be able to name every single thing, or would you forget something? Would you be able to rank each item in perfect, successive order of how much you love each thing? Would you be able to tell me exactly *why* you love it and be 100 percent certain you love *it*, not just *telling people* that you love it? Could you be sure that you have not defaulted into saying that for so long that it's become a knee-jerk, preprogrammed response and not an actual feeling?

That's why we're here to answer the ten questions that get at: What do you really love?

For a more official scoring, you can take my seventeen-question lovability index for free at alexdripchak.com. There you can see if something is just a job, a potential career, or a true calling.

Knowing *why* you do something isn't simply a nice-to-do, touchy-feely, let's-all-hold-hands-and-sing-Kumbaya exercise in emotion; it's a necessity.

If your why isn't strong enough to weather a few storms or setbacks, you'll grow embittered, jaded, disgusted, angry, disappointed, sad, or downright nihilistic. If left unchecked, this can grow to a point where your productivity takes a massive hit. Of course, you can do what many do and self-soothe with vacations, family time, material possessions, or maybe even a new role or job, but this isn't weatherproof. The minute another storm comes, your house is in tatters. You need to ask yourself: *Is my why hurricane proof?*

Will it stand a layoff, a bad boss, an unexpected RIF or economic downturn, financial pressure, a literal or metaphorical hurricane?

Now, if your house isn't standing intact after this storm scenario, don't panic. Ask yourself, *How can I add some layers of reinforcement? Or How can I build myself a bomb shelter (e.g., passion project or side job) in case the house does fall down?*

There's so much talk about burnout, and the surest way to protect against burnout is to have something you love doing day in and day out. It's hackneyed and trite to say, so here are some self-reflection questions to challenge you to know for sure if your "something you love" is only good or truly great:

1. When working on "it," does time fly by for you?
2. Will you go past tired, hungry, thirsty to finish your idea, your session, your flow?
3. Does talking about it bring a smile to your face?
    a. A lift in spirits?
    b. A rise in posture?
    c. A boost in physical well-being?
4. Do you "have to" go to it or do you "get to" go to it?
5. Are the mundane tasks boring, point-in-time actions (e.g., "I'm cementing rocks.") or foundational and purposeful conduits to something greater (e.g., "I'm building a cathedral."[25])?
6. What's easier: Getting into a rhythm? Or getting knocked out of one?
7. Who do you do the work for?
8. When working, are you: inattentive, trying to concentrate, focused, indistractable?
9. If you were independently wealthy, would you still work on it? If so, how many hours per week?
10. If you were structuring your ideal day and could do anything you wanted, would you work on this endeavor?

In summation: *Why* isn't optional. The strength of your why shapes how successful your result. It's not correlation; it's causation. ∎

35. MINIMIZE PARTAKING IN NEGATIVITY

As Jay Shetty says in his book *Think like a Monk*: Time spent complaining or criticizing is time you could have spent focused on improving yourself. Or to put it simply—*Negativity negates productivity*.[26]

It's an extremely powerful passage. We have many sections on the brevity of life, and now we have some powerful guidance on how to spend our time. To reframe Shetty's message, negativity gives us a tick in the loss column, whereas a focus on growth and improvement gives us one in the win column. What's your record this week?

You may ask, "What about the moments when the difficult topic needs to be broached?"

Before you start complaining, criticizing, or critiquing, ask yourself, *Is this a topic we can or want to address?* Oftentimes that alone is enough to stop the action in its tracks.

If you answered yes, continue this exercise by asking, *Will going about this negativity result in something productive? If yes, ask yourself, How will we establish when we've moved off from problem-solving and into pure complaining?* A final step is to determine the amount of time when complaining goes too far, for example the thirty minutes I mentioned earlier in this book as the threshold when being negative actually reduces your problem-solving capabilities.

Assign someone to act as your positivity defense attorney in the process, objecting with all the favorite TV and movie phrases.

What if, when asking yourself that second question, you thought, *No, it would not be a productive discussion*. Double-check by asking yourself, *How could we reframe, reapproach, or review it so that it is productive?*

If you determined there is no reframe or reapproach and have confirmed this conversation is not worth having at all, you may have saved yourself from a potential deluge into negativity, but you're not done just yet as you still need to consider your conversation partner.

First ask, is there value in being empathetic to the person you're speaking with? If yes, find a way to listen, support, and subsequently shift (LSS) onto more positive topics. If no, is your relationship at risk if you do not deluge into the negativity? If yes, ask yourself, is a potential downside risk of this relationship worthwhile? If yes, stand firm and politely avoid the topic. If no, abide by LSS again. If your relationship is not at risk, stop the discussion.

If all this writing in paragraph form made your head spin, don't worry—I've put it all in a fun decision-tree graphic. ■

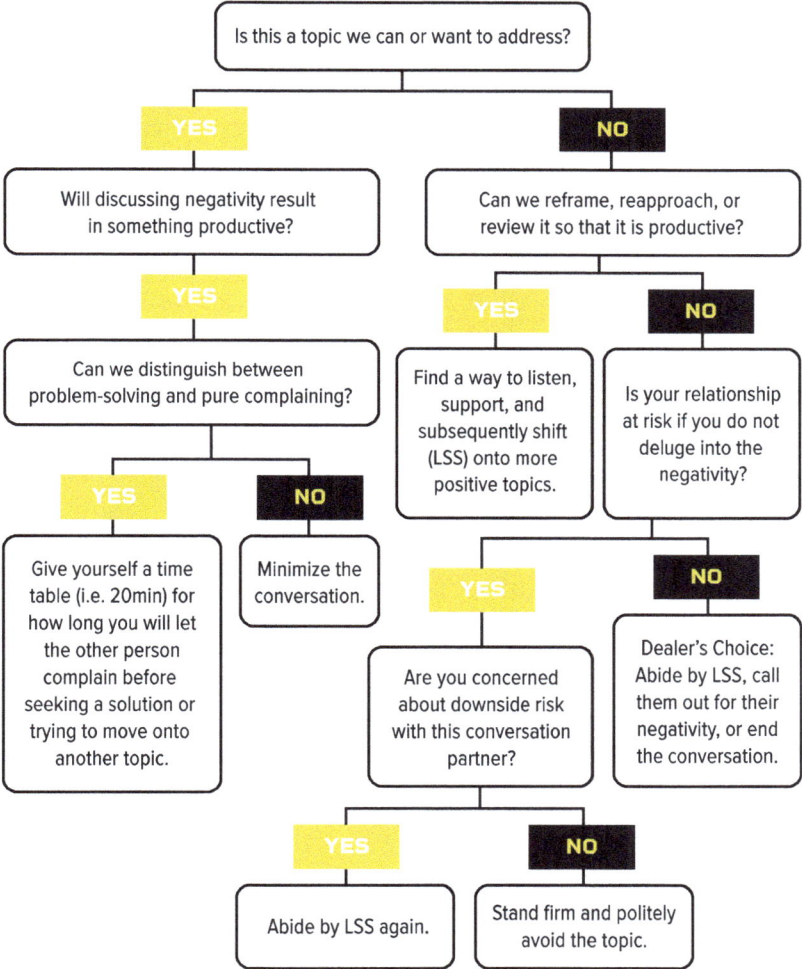

Is this a topic we can or want to address?

YES → Will discussing negativity result in something productive?

YES → Can we distinguish between problem-solving and pure complaining?

YES → Give yourself a time table (i.e. 20min) for how long you will let the other person complain before seeking a solution or trying to move onto another topic.

NO → Minimize the conversation.

NO → Can we reframe, reapproach, or review it so that it is productive?

YES → Find a way to listen, support, and subsequently shift (LSS) onto more positive topics.

NO → Is your relationship at risk if you do not deluge into the negativity?

YES → Are you concerned about downside risk with this conversation partner?

YES → Abide by LSS again.

NO → Stand firm and politely avoid the topic.

NO → Dealer's Choice: Abide by LSS, call them out for their negativity, or end the conversation.

34. IMAGINE EVERYONE AND NO ONE ARE WATCHING

AS RIVETING AS Practice 85 is, that advice works only for the moments you want the spotlight or want the confidence that passage brings to bear. But how about if you want more consistent productivity without the attention?

It starts with finding a place where you can exist without being the center of attention. You're not on stage, not presenting to an audience, not in a conference room. Great—now we've got the spotlight off. But before you retreat into a quiet, isolated room, office, or cubicle, we still need to be surrounded by others, otherwise we may slack off.

So the question is, what's a place where both everyone is watching you and no one? Does this Goldilocks of productivity environments exist? Well, for many, it's a quiet library. In a library, if you do something dramatic, you're likely to get eyes on you. But if you stick to your work, you're left alone. It's that ideal middle ground we've been looking for.

Harness this setting: Use the nearby eyes as an accountability tactic, and the peace of mind that no one is directly looking at you to enable you to get into a rhythm. You're not thinking about them because, frankly, you don't need to; they will look over if you need help.

Get into your groove and open up a world of limitless possibilities while in your world of one. ■

33. MINIMIZE PURE ENTERTAINMENT VALUE ACTIVITIES

TIME MANAGEMENT

THESE ARE THE real drags on productivity—the items whose presence, and mere existence, you have a really hard time justifying being in your life.

They don't contribute to your fealty, your family, your fulfillment, your friends, or your future.

The only F they achieve is an F for failure.

So, what are the lowest-value-add activities, you may ask.

Instagram comments on influencer accounts, YouTube videos, video games, scrolling time, Netflix/Hulu/Disney+/the other TV apps—they all take us away. Or if you're me, an Achilles's heel could be lists of hypothetical scenarios that'll never happen. Like, who would win a basketball series—Team '80s (Magic Johnson, Michael Jordan, Larry Bird, Moses Malone, Hakeem Olajuwon) or Team 2020s (Steph Curry, Kevin Durant, LeBron James, Giannis Antetokounmpo, Nikola Jokić). The suspense builds as one can argue that each side has five top twenty players of all time, and surprisingly only one team has a unanimous MVP. And no, it's not who you think it is or even your second choice. It's my favorite player of all time: Steph Curry.

Between the hypothetical, the argument, and the fun facts, you can see how easy it is to get sidetracked.

I saw a great quote on Instagram (ironically enough): "One who lacks purpose, distracts themselves with pleasure." And this quote is profoundly true—my days when I can't center on my purpose, those are my days distracted with pleasure. Applying it further, those people I know living a purposeful life are steadfast, and those I know centering on pleasure have little to center their lives.

Now for those reading who say, "Well, I haven't discovered or found my purpose yet," that's not an excuse or a get-out-of-jail-free card to distract yourself with pleasure. Au contraire, my friend. It's all the more reason to seek out what your purpose is. Throw yourself into what you *like* to see if it matures into something you *love*, and that love you discover might just be your God-given, higher force, purpose in life.

Now, in the title of this section I say "minimize" as opposed to "eliminate" for two primary reasons: (1) to prevent burnout, and (2) to prevent yourself from becoming addicted to work, which would likely lead to burnout, if not something worse—beginning to dislike what you used to love. Take any kid who enjoyed an activity (sports, music, chess, etc.) at a young age but was pushed too hard, burned out, and began to resent the game. We all know at least one. So this practice is an interesting oxymoron: equal parts high importance in its lesson and low importance in its application. Put simply, a little bit of entertainment keeps us sane, but too much can derail our life.

To paraphrase the original productivity expert, Stephen Covey, in his lauded *The 7 Habits of Highly Effective People*, technology is a great servant, but a terrible master.[27]

In other words, the difference between technology being a help or hindrance comes down to purpose and intentionality.

If TV is a reward or much-needed break—great. If it runs beyond that and starts to feel purposeless, then it's now in control. This is where intentionality comes into play. When watching television, ask yourself, *What will I gain from watching? How much time do I want to spend on this?* Or for events you're watching, *What moments do I want to capture?* You may quickly realize that it's really about the final moments more so than the entire event. After all, it's the finishes people remember, and for any other highlights, you can catch them on Twitter, YouTube, or SportsCenter.

The following is a progressive step chart to help you combat watching television, beginning with it as a significant problem and ending with it as something to tweak or refine for maximal focus:

1. If it's on in the background, turn it on **mute**.
2. If it's on in the background, turn it **off**.
3. Turn it on and flip through the channels. Only **if** you find something you're excited about, watch it.
4. For what looks appealing, ask yourself, Do I **need** to watch all of this?
5. If you opt to watch all of it, what can you do during **downtime** or commercials?
6. If you opt to watch all of it, what can you do during the show itself that doesn't distract from the show? (e.g., cleaning up, **dishes**, etc.)
   a. If watching all of it, is it the primary, equal, or secondary focus? Your TV volume should match your desired focus level, with primary focus equating to entertainment level volume, equal focus equating to audible volume, and secondary focus equating to barely audible volume (to

only catch the program volume, intonation, or celebratory changes as **markers** to tune in).

7. If you opt to watch some of it, set a time **limit** and use a timer or other mechanism to ensure you keep to your goal.
8. Only turn on the TV for events you're specifically, **highly** interested in.
9. **Repeat** steps three to seven for special shows/events.
10. Set a limit for what you'll spend time watching—say, three focal points per season/**quarter**.
    a. For me this is a rotation of what's in season between Boston College, the Golden State Warriors, NFL RedZone/Sunday Ticket, three **select** PGA Tour events, and one to two TV shows at a time.
11. Can you **listen** to your favorite shows instead of watching them? If so, can you combine activities? Say, driving to/from somewhere and listening to the game/event in the car? Or listen while you're working out on the treadmill?
12. Cut your shortlist/refine it further. Did you **actively** miss watching something you cut, or only when someone mentioned it? Or, best of all, did you find that you didn't miss it at all? ▪

32. PURSUE MORE SECOND- AND THIRD-ORDER EFFECTS

MOTIVATION AND ALIGNMENT

PURSUING SOMETHING that provides immediate benefit(s) is easy. Take the entertainment you get by watching Netflix versus going to the gym. At the beginning of going to the gym, you're tired, out of breath, might have a cramp—the whole thing is not fun. It's not Netflix. But the second-order effects are the endorphin rush and overall feel-good experience from exercise. The third-order effect is a healthier lifestyle. What this shows us is, if you put in the work on the front end, it pays off downstream.

Purpose aside, if the task itself provides immediate joy, chances are it's not good for your long term.

As Mark Manson talks about in his book *The Subtle Art of Not Giving a F*ck*, success comes from conquering the associated negative experience, or as he calls it, the backwards law. His top example is a familiar one: The pain you endure in the gym results in better health.[28]

Both second/third-order effects and the backwards law teach us the same thing: Life is about putting effort into the difficult to accomplish a truly positive result. Therefore, we need to be laser-focused on where we place our intention. As Dr. Andrew Huberman puts it: "The only thing we can truly control is where we place our attention and where we place our effort. Choose wisely."[29] So, if you can put your attention and effort toward doing the hard thing(s), that's a win.

One of those hard things we can do is not only pursue the second- and third-order effects but also delay indulging in the first-order effects, as legendary billionaire hedge fund manager Ray Dalio tells us in his book *Principles*. Ray puts it well when he says, "Quite often the first-order consequences are the temptations that cost us what we really want, and sometimes they are the barriers that stand in our way."[30]

Think of the famed marshmallow experiment(s). Stanford researchers did studies on more than five hundred children aged three and a half to five years, nine months and said they could have one marshmallow right away or two marshmallows if they waited fifteen minutes—the choice was theirs. Those who were able to wait demonstrated higher success levels in academics, health, and measures of life success. While the study had its challenges and naysayers, the theme of positive impact from delayed gratification has been proven in this study and again in similar research studies and the real world.[31] Take the stock market. Every year the stock market has intrayear losses at some point. Yet its yearly performance has been positive thirty out of the last forty-one years, and it's never had a period where an investment has lost money over a twenty-year time horizon; more often than not, it shows a gain that outpaces inflation at a rate of nearly four to one.

The lesson? Delayed gratification pays off. In business, in money, in habit formation, in marshmallows. ■

31. SUBSTITUTE, OR REPLACE, BAD HABITS

HAVE YOU EVER given someone profound and applicable advice only to hear, "I don't have (the) time."

Or perhaps it was more politely phrased as, "Yeah, I'd love to do that but I just don't have the time."

How did you feel? Frustrated at this trite excuse? Unappreciated for trying to help? Disappointed to have them get so close to changing their life for the better, only to keep perpetuating the problem?

We've all felt one, if not all three, of these ways.

So instead of ending the conversation there and letting them go on their way, how can you get them to override this thinking and take a progressive step?

Perhaps you can try something to the effect of, "I totally get it—days are already jam-packed as we try to stay above water multitasking across a million different things, and a day has the audacity to still be the same twenty-four hours it always has been! Finding new time really does look impossible. Instead of trying to find new time, is there something you currently have on your plate that you want to get rid of or reduce? Could you reallocate some of this time toward developing this new plan?"

The end goal is to get them to realize that the time is already being allocated, so someone doesn't have to find *new* time, they just have to review, reframe, and reallocate their time or simply *redirect* their impulses.

For instance, when you want to lie on the couch or take a nap, go exercise. After all, the goal is oftentimes the same: cultivating a revitalized energy.

For a more advanced version of this thinking, when you're craving a slice of pizza, eat an apple. With exercising replacing napping, the goal can be the same, but I don't think anyone would say the goal of eating pizza and eating an apple is the same. As great as envy apples are, they don't compare to pizza, not in the Tri-State area, at least. So here, the goals are somewhat, but not as, similar.

Level 3 thinking would be finding ways to fully replace a bad habit. For instance, let's say every Friday is pizza Friday for you, but you want to start a diet. If you replace the time you allocate toward going to your favorite pizzeria with going for a run and calling it Fitness Friday instead, it's a great reallocation of time, but now both the act and the goals are completely different than the original.

So before you jump to Level 3 like so many people attempt to do in their New Year's resolutions, which fizzle out 88 percent of the time, try working your way up through smaller, simpler, and more closely related impulse redirection first.[32] Once you get good at replacing the similar goals, then you can look to make these big jumps. ■

30. LEVERAGE "TEMPTATION BUNDLING"

HABIT FORMATION

ENTERTAINMENT HAS become a higher priority than education in our society. Inflationary forces keep making the cost of education balloon, while technological advances have made entertainment more and more affordable. In the last forty-two years, TVs have had negative inflation forty-one times, meaning that they almost always continue to get cheaper, or to put it another way, more and more accessible.[33]

And it isn't just TV that is showing signs of availability inevitability. According to a 2024 Pew Research Center survey, 90 percent of US adults own a smartphone.[34] This is more than double the percentage of smartphone owners in 2011, when only 35 percent of adults owned a smartphone. This may sound rather elementary for our society, but consider the following: In an early 2024 CNBC report, just under half of Americans had less than $500 in savings, and 60 percent had less than $500 in checking.[35] This means that a large portion of those smartphone owners don't even have enough in their checking and savings combined to afford the iPhone 14 Pro Max outright. Entertainment has become so ingrained in our society that those who don't physically have the dollars and cents to pay for it still have it in their hands.

In addition to telling us a lot of folks might need to rethink their finances, this tells us we need to do our best to battle against the powerful force of entertainment. Fortunately, for those moments when you can't seem to muster up the energy to battle against it, you can bundle it.

Enter Ronan Byrne, an electrical engineering student in Dublin who showed if you can't beat 'em, bundle 'em.[36] Ronan is the man you can thank next time you go to the gym and watch your favorite shows while you work out, provided you do, indeed, work out. Ronan programmed his bicycle to only allow him to watch Netflix if he kept pedaling. It was a genius invention and one we get to benefit from now frequently. If you aren't a gym-goer, other ways to take advantage of this concept include:

1. Only watching TV while cleaning the apartment
2. Only having dessert after going for a postdinner walk outside.
3. Sorting through mail (a task I hate) while outside on a balcony or porch to get some sunlight and outdoors time.

Earlier I mentioned an app that's trying to capitalize on this temptation bundling concept by tying scrolling time to exercise. In order to use the apps you want to restrict, you must have enough time stored up via push-ups, steps, or squats. If you don't, you have to do more exercises or you simply don't get to go on that app. There's no skip or "extra time" feature like on social media platforms or even like those on your phone settings. It is a very clever concept that combines many productivity maxims into one app. ■

29. SEEK OUT CORRECTIVE FEEDBACK

HABIT FORMATION

ONE OF THE hardest things about the corporate world I've seen over the last ten years is a shift away from feedback. The sad truth of the matter is that feedback, criticism, or anything that could be construed as tough to hear often only comes during a RIF (reduction in force), layoff, or termination. This unfortunate correlation makes it even more challenging to want to seek feedback, for if feedback is only given in life's toughest, most traumatic moments, why would you want it?

This entangled perception fused with greater corporate sensitivity, performance discussion backfires, generational shifts, and managerial discomfort or disagreement with performance review systems has amalgamated to put performance reviews at, or near, an all-time low. This has been studied extensively at HBR, CEB, SHRM, Fast Company, Willis Towers Watson, and several others, and each study points back to two things: We are at, or near, an all-time low in both use of performance reviews and recognized benefit of performance reviews to individuals and organizations. And worse yet, this trend shows no signs of slowing down or reversing course; so what is there to do?

While the traditional way of receiving feedback via the performance review may be dead at one-third of companies and dying at many more, there are many opportunities to seek feedback yourself.[37] The beauty of this self-starter approach is the more you receive feedback, the less likely it is to hurt. And the earlier you ask for it, the more you'll get, the less awkward it'll be, and less "tied to your future at this company" it'll both feel and be.

Yes, it may be painful or uncomfortable, but it's worth it. While it may be tempting to try and take the easy road by seeking informational or outcome feedback, resist this urge. To be most aware of each feedback type, let's define them, starting with informational feedback, the third level of feedback.

- **Informational feedback (Level 3):** Feedback that happens immediately, or shortly after, an action or catalyst. This feedback can point to a problem but gives very little when it comes to solutions.

- **Outcome feedback (Level 4):** Feedback that takes place shortly after the end of an event. It tells you where you went wrong, and how/why it went that way. Outcome feedback is a deeper dive into informational feedback.

- **Corrective feedback (Level 5):** Feedback that takes place soon after the action or event is complete and provides what outcome feedback does, plus gives you a roadmap for how to not only fix issues in the future but also plan for recognizing warning signs or spotting potential pitfalls before they occur.

I've started at Level 3 because that's where anything resembling actionable feedback begins. Level 1 to me is generic rhetorical questions disguised as feedback, like "any questions?" and Level 2 is another more commonly built-in postmortem or postcall analysis where folks chitchat about a call and its occurrences, as opposed to any areas of improvements, action steps, or concrete feedback.

While Level 3 and Level 4 feedback are beneficial to track, people applauding, looking disinterested, or leaving can be good, implied directional feedback, but it isn't concrete. Your job is to find what is. Ask for feedback or advice. Don't seek commentary and don't ask, "What did you think?" or "Did you like it?" Don't lead the witness in a positive direction, because if they were about to say something constructive, they are likely to switch to something more supportive. If anything, lead them toward the negative with questions like "What could I have done better?" or "To make this even more effective/impactful next time, what would you suggest I do in the future?" This will get you to solicit not only the unvarnished opinion, but also the most productive one. ◾

28. AUDIT YOUR TIME: DO YOUR ACTIONS MATCH YOUR VALUES?

<mark>TIME MANAGEMENT</mark>

We as human beings have a tendency to overestimate how much we do. I know I'm not immune.

We say we work eight hours a day; however, do you know what the prominent studies show? *Inc.* magazine puts the number at two hours and fifty-three minutes in their study,[38] Blind at four hours,[39] and Zippia at four hours and twelve minutes.[40] So according to these studies, at best, the average worker produces for half the day. If you think that sounds like an exaggeration, consider the bathroom breaks, water cooler chats, texting, going out to get lunch, eating lunch, and so many more activities that many people engage in, like personal phone calls, checking social media, and shopping. And—the pièce de résistance—the average person spends twenty-six minutes per day at their job…looking for another job![41]

These are just the things someone can do for active disengagement. There are many forms of hidden disengagement like childcare obligations and other family situations, travel problems, housing, health issues, and the accompanying stress and anxiety of each respective challenge someone faces.

One of my colleagues at Bright Horizons puts it eloquently when he says many companies think about absenteeism—losing people to unexpected out-of-offices—but what they should also think about is presenteeism—which focuses more on getting the most out of your people while they are at work and giving them the tools, resources, and peace of mind to do just that.[42]

While companies increase their awareness and focus on presenteeism, how can you shine a light on presenteeism in both your own personal and professional lives? It begets the question: Are you really working hard on your passions and purpose, or are you distracted (actively or passively) by unrelated things?

You won't truly know until you assess. And while it may feel self-assuring or prideful to say you're not a part of this issue and then proceed to continue to artificially inflate these numbers, the only person you'll be lying to is yourself. It's an overused saying, but put another way, misreporting your actual productivity will cost you years, if not decades, of lost opportunity, and no matter how long you live, that time will never be truly recovered.

So what should you do?

Perform a Free Time-to-Values Alignment Assessment

Start by tracking how much free time you had in a day and do that over the course of a seven-day week. There are sixteen waking hours in a day. When you subtract an eight-hour workday, two hours of commuting/hygiene upkeep, and two hours of meals, that's likely to leave you (and many others) with four hours per day of "free time" or twenty-eight hours per week. This roughly translates to *each hour you spend being 4 percent of your weekly free time, or each fifteen-minute window being 1 percent. If you tracked it in grading terms, would your free time assessment receive a passing grade? For many of us, I imagine the answer is no, and that's OK. When you see what your time is actually going to—not what you aspirationally desire, socially exaggerate, or mentally delude—you'll have the power to improve, if not fully course-correct.*

There was a quote by Seneca that got me reflecting on how to further refine this free time-to-values alignment activity. The quote reads: "It is not that we have a short time to live, but that we waste a lot of it."[43]

If time were stored like we store food in a refrigerator, how much are you throwing in the trash can?

This quote got me thinking about not only how much time is wasted, but also how much time is spent, or misspent, on social conformities; what we would define as insanity (doing the same thing over and over and expecting a different result); and overindexed time on substandard outcomes (like that ninety-minute meeting that could have been nine minutes or, even worse, a nine-line email).

A lot of this is beyond our control, but it inspired me to create the chart that follows. Of the 168 hours in a week (112 waking hours), how many do you place in each bucket, where can you improve these numbers with your inputs, and are you happy with these current and proposed figures? ▪

Monday	Tuesday	Wednesday	Thursday	Friday	Saturday	Sunday
Maximized: (Operated at 90-plus percent and/or worked on what you want to be remembered for and/or won't ever regret)						
Utilized: (Operated at 65-plus percent and/or accomplished necessary tasks for the well-being of yourself, those you love, and/or those who rely upon you)						
Sacrificed/Conformed: (Time spent against your will and judgment, against your loves and purpose)						
Wasted: (Time spent on trivialities, unnecessary anxiety, or prolonged dwelling; tasks that produce nothing for others and/or no fulfillment for you)						
Unrefined: (Time spent dillydallying, procrastinating, daydreaming, or otherwise doing anything that's outside of listening or solutioning toward your task and its intended result)						

27. FOCUS ON VALUE PRODUCERS, NOT FEEL GOODS

MOTIVATION AND ALIGNMENT

LET'S SAY YOU HAVE the energy you need. You've channeled it into your work. You have no problem with procrastination or getting started. You can even sustain the energy throughout and finish the work feeling great. To make matters even more exciting, you're able to replicate this effort consistently. You do all this and still fail to advance yourself forward. Everything came together—the stars aligned—and you're left with next to nothing to show for it; how is this even possible?

Oftentimes we can get focused on production, but it's not the right kind of production, and you're no better off than those still sitting at the starting line. It's the things that feel good that unknowingly knock us off course. I fall victim to this one a lot more than I care to admit. I see a list I don't agree with and have to make my own. A curiosity—like I wonder how many countries I can name off the top of my head—takes control over me, and before I know it, 9:00 p.m. turns into 11:00 p.m. in a flash.

If you also struggle with staying centered on what matters most, try to center back on Brendan Burchard's concept of PQO, or prolific quality output. You should be spending at least 40 percent of your time on your PQO. And if you're not, you should stop and ask yourself these six important questions until you get a yes. If you don't get a yes, then you need to treat that activity like entertainment, because that's solely what it's providing.

1. Am I doing this just because it feels good to me, or will it realistically produce something for others?
2. Do those "others" want this?
3. If not, can it be rearranged, repackaged, or repurposed into something people want and will pay for?
4. If not, is this something that will realistically open doors for me to build toward my purpose, profession, or personal production?
5. Is this something that at a minimum will be a conversation topic among friends and family?
6. Is this something that will make it into the light of day or be kept in my own files for the foreseeable future?

If it's not producing for you, doesn't have potential to power your future, or isn't poised to be part of your discussions, treat it as entertainment.

It's very easy to fill up your schedule with the feel goods and lose track of time both in the moment and in totality. This is especially problematic because time is the one thing you lose that you never get back. Good health and habits may grant you greater longevity, or you may be fortunate to get a second chance at the very opportunity you missed previously, but this present moment, the one you're enjoying right now as you read this book, you'll never get again.

Fill up your schedule with those tasks that will produce, or have the realistic potential to produce, the most fruit for you. ■

26. CONSCIOUSLY TURN OFF YOUR AUTOPILOT

ACCORDING TO RESEARCH from the Max Planck Institute, as much as 95 percent of our day is decided by our subconscious mind, or to put it another way, it's mostly spent on autopilot.[44] Even the most conservative studies, like the 2010 study from Harvard, put the number around 47 percent.[45] Forty-seven to 95 percent of our days aren't even conscious, intentional choices?! How is this possible?! Well, let's review.

You get up, check your phone, brush your teeth, and shower. *All autopilot.* Get dressed, make/grab some food, and drive to work. Again, *all autopilot.* You get coffee, work, chat with colleagues, and have meetings. *Half autopilot.* Get lunch or eat at your desk—most of which is *autopiloting.* Finish your work, get in your car, go home. *Half autopilot.* Watch TV, make dinner, ask questions about someone's day. *Mostly autopilot.* Then get ready for bed—*autopilot.*

Forty-seven to 95 percent autopilot? Well, we're just about smack in the middle of that range with 70 percent being autopilot in this sample day above.

So what can you do? Begin by increasing your awareness: How much of your day was spent intentionally? How much was accidental or reactive?

Clearly the default is accidental, so we need to check ourselves not just into awareness but into hyperpresence.

We need to clue in, turn on, override, activate, or otherwise change course to get to intentional. This sobering observation makes this principle even more challenging. Every moment you are not deciding on the intentional, you are defaulting to the autopilot. You are defaulting to the accidental. The way the wind blows. The reactionary. The uncontrolled. The "my life will pass me by if I don't opt in." *Break it.* ■

OBSERVATION

Autopilot is strongest when our energy is lowest. If you're not getting the sleep you need, the breaks your body requires, the exercise your brain asks for, then you're at greater risk to fall victim to, and stay a victim of, autopilot.

SECTION CHECK-IN

My Three to Five Potential Practices:

1. _____

_____

2. _____

_____

3. _____

_____

4. _____

_____

5. _____

_____

25–1

ACHIEVING GREATNESS

25. ATTACH IMMEDIATE GRATIFICATION TO LONG-TERM GOALS AND IMMEDIATE CONSEQUENCES TO TRANSGRESSIONS

HABIT FORMATION

OUR NEED FOR dopamine in the days of social media, you could argue, is at an all-time high, and the clarity of long-term anything—never mind goals—is harder and harder to envision and subsequently harder to make tangible. Therefore, you need to find ways to reward yourself for meaningful progress. For progressions, you can make a vacation jar, or conversely, for transgressions, you can create a swear jar of sorts—money you will give, donate, or take away from fun activities when you slip up.

Dr. Julie Smith takes this a step further to say you should not only use external reward incentives but also self-appreciation gestures, like a pat on the back or congratulating yourself. As Adam Grant says in his book *Hidden Potential*, the most effective way to accomplish goals is by breaking them into small pieces to continue to see progress.[1]

This process also works for anything negative. You punish, penalize, and track results over time and make sure to give yourself an *immediate demerit for any slipups*. Channel what I'll call the "pulled over" mindset. You know that feeling when you just got a speeding ticket? You have an authority figure with a big hat giving a ticket. Lights are flashing, sirens are sounding. Everyone's looking at you on the side of the road—it's a very public, very obvious punishment. What happens after that? You drive slower, proving the ticket worked, for at least the next ten minutes, but maybe ten hours, ten days, or, especially if you received points on your license, maybe ten months. Maybe forever. It's a very effective way to get us to change behavior. It builds commitment because it stays ingrained in our memory for a while. We need more of these slap-on-the-wrist pullovers in life, as we have a tendency to let ourselves off easy because life is tough enough. While true, without a punishment, we will continue to miss. As James Clear says, and I repeat again, missing once is an accident, and missing twice is the start of a new habit.

And to prevent or punish that missing-twice attitude, we need clear markers of missing an input goal. Most likely you don't have a police officer to call you out publicly, so a more applicable idea is to think of increasingly more severe punishments for each day missed. The following is an example:

How to Ensure Missing One Day Doesn't Turn into Missing a Week

Day 1: Empty your jar and reflect on the broken streak.

Day 2: Notify your accountability partner that you've missed again.

Day 3: Put $20 in the "Buy rival sports team gear if I don't restart my habit" jar.

Day 4: Purchase a hat, shirt, or some other wearable gear of your bitter rival.

Day 5: Wear said hat or shirt of your bitter rival.

Day 6: I think the first five days are bad enough and hopefully you don't need this day. But if you do…post on social media a photo of you wearing your bitter rival's gear. ■

24. AUDIT YOUR LIFE'S RELATIONSHIPS

MOTIVATION AND ALIGNMENT

YOU'VE HEARD ABOUT positive peer groups, and you'll get my take on how to refine that for maximal efficacy in a few sections, but perhaps an even more important assessment is to ask yourself: *Do I know everyone's current impact on, or desired intentions for, my life?*

It sounds strange to say, but the majority of people either don't want you to—or don't care if you—actually succeed. And no, I'm not just talking about the informal, general, outside world "people." I'm talking about acquaintances. I'm talking about colleagues. I'm even talking about family and friends. James Altucher in his (excellent) book *Skip the Line* talks about this and paints a vivid picture when he says there are a few things you need to realize, four of which, I believe, are just what the productivity doctor ordered:

1. Nobody wakes up thinking, *I'm going to make someone famous today.*
2. Most people don't care about their jobs (so why would they care about yours?)
3. Many people think you should have to earn your way or pay your dues largely because that's how they had to do it.
4. People are frustrated with their own lives, dealing with their own problems.[2]

What you need to do is start categorizing the people in your life into buckets. Now I'm not saying to kick anyone out of your life or to categorize them as this label forever, but right now, take a hard look at the following four categories and ask yourself who in your life falls into which categories. I've put them on a continuum, as not everyone will fall neatly into one category.

Downers	Neutrals	Builders	Risers

Downers: People who are any *one* or more of the following:
- Negative about their life and yours
- Unsupportive—either actively or openly

- Consistently seeking to remind you of past failures, difficulties, or times of your more unpolished self
- Actively seeking to knock you off your desired course or mire you down in life's trivialities
- Sucking or draining life out of you, leeching off success, or antagonizing pursuits of progress

Important note: Downers don't have to be negative people. While oftentimes they are negative, the term downer shouldn't refer to the subject, but instead to the impact they have on their audience. Put simply, they are people who keep you down. Keep an eye out for the happy downers, or *veiled saboteurs*, in your life, as they are far more dangerous than the negatives.

Neutrals: The passably apathetic majority, folks who
- Indulge in surface-level enjoyments and discussions
- Have basic focal points, are nonreflective, are most comfortable with lots of small talk and banter, and pursue conversation that is reactionary and observational
- Have minimal impact on what you define as your most passionate pursuits, which are neither markedly better nor worse with them in your life

Builder (Upper)s: Those who
- Take an active interest
- Seek to understand before being understood
- Ask, engage, clarify, and help refine
- Are complimentary and self-esteem boosting, making you feel better about yourself and what you want to become

Risers: Those who
- Are supportive of your endeavors and actively pursuing their own
- Do not know jealousy, envy, or bitterness toward others
- Are people of significant growth and are constantly iterating on their own evolution
- Seek to connect you to others, to value actions over words, to focus on driving positive contributions beyond their own small, personal circle/world

Now before you place people into buckets, first ask yourself these five questions:

1. When I'm talking about what matters to me, does this person passively listen, engage, support, or advocate for me?
   a. Passively listen
   b. Engage openly/deeply
   c. Support/encourage
   d. Actively advocate/advance

2. Over the course of your relationship, has this person accomplished, or attempted to accomplish, anything of nonstandard personal or professional progression?
   a. Yes
   b. No
   c. Not sure

3. When sharing an idea, is this person pessimistic, gradualistic, holistic, optimistic, or idealistic? Circle your answer.

4. When getting together with this person, do they seek to:
   a. Showcase any self-perceived advantages they have
   b. Better themselves/the collective group
   c. Meet others where they're at
   d. Bring people down to their desired level
   e. Bring people down below their level

5. If you were to share a polite, cause-based accomplishment on social media, would this person behind closed doors say:
   a. This is amazing—others need to know about this
   b. Good for them—that's awesome
   c. OK (and skip to next post)
   d. (Eye roll) Here we go with this... _____
   e. OMG—why is their life so good?!
   f. Why do they have to share this?

If your answers looked like

1. B–D
2. A
3. 3 or 4 (5 is OK)
4. B or C
5. A or B

then you, my friend, have at least a builder, if not a riser—someone to cherish, as well as to continue to cultivate—in your life. Most people—my initial estimate would be somewhere around 75 percent of people—are neutrals. And that's perfectly OK! It's just the way life goes as people are tired, depressed, struggling, selfish, or anything else that keeps them from helping you more. I know I'd only be categorized as a neutral to many, but I'm also proud to be a riser to many others.

It's almost impossible to be a riser to everyone. What you need to do is find potential risers and see if you can get close enough to them to build a true riser relationship. Conversely, while risers can be neutrals or perhaps even builders to some, downers cannot be risers. The inherent pulling down attitude is in direct opposition to the growth and absence of envy or jealousy indicative of a riser. So in the situations where you can choose relationships, avoid downers as much as possible. Recognize and respect that most will be neutrals. Expect your friends and family to at least be builders. Seek out and grow the few possible risers out there.

In other words: Avoid. Recognize. Expect. Seek. Grow.

A-R-E S-G.

ARE (you) Seeking Growth? ∎

23. SPEND ONE TO NINE MINUTES ELEVATING YOUR HEART RATE

IF ONLY WE had a dollar every time someone said they don't have enough time to exercise. But since we don't get a dollar for enduring that ear-sore, we endeavor onward. Perhaps the lack of hand-me-out dollars in the world is the very reason why many of you are reading this book! While thirty minutes (or more) of daily exercise is something I will fight tooth and nail for, consider this passage my olive branch.

Whether it's been when I'm crunched for time, or when I'm looking to optimize mental acuity, one question has come to mind more than any other: *How much exercise time is enough to notice benefits?*

Setting out on my research for this topic was a bit like doing the limbo—how low can you go? I found lots of proof of the benefits of twenty minutes of exercise and equally as much at fifteen minutes. It was around ten minutes that this researching limbo got a bit harder. Surprisingly, the limbo bar was able to stretch even further with proof that went all the way down to showing benefits after just three minutes of exercise! With articles in *The Washington Post*, *The New York Times*, and *Time* magazine, I was encouraged.

However, the encouragement didn't stop at the three-minute, research-backed level. Brain health and energy expert Jim Kwik says it takes only one to three minutes of elevated heart rate activity to notice clearer thinking, and it's why he opens his days with short intense exercises like burpees, jumping jacks, and various other calisthenics.[3] And it's not just Jim who subscribes to this; our other frequently cited expert, Brendon Burchard, does too.[4] And I believe them because I, too, live it. I have a hard time existing, or languishing, in anything less than 70 percent of my optimal brain energy state, so much so that I seek to change that state immediately.

So, what are some of the quickest ways to a changed state of increased mental acuity? Here's a list of strategies in order of decreasing time commitments that I've found to personally make a difference and that are worth trying for yourself:

1. Nine minutes jogging at an elevated pace

2. Five minutes of intense Peloton(ing)
3. Two minutes of speed/jumping rope
4. One minute on Jacob's Ladder (if you haven't heard of this—look it up. Or at least imagine the scene in *Rocky IV* when they show Rocky climbing up a hill full of snow—sometimes that's how this feels.)
5. One minute sprinting at or near full speed

Now, while this may sound easy, when I say just a couple minutes, this isn't for anything inside the comfort zone. What I mean by this is don't confuse jogging for sprinting, casual stair climbing for Jacob's Ladder, or reading your book while on the stationary bike for a HIIT (high-impact interval training) Peloton ride. Giving it your all could look like: double-digit MPH running, 100-plus stairs per minute on Jacob's Ladder, 250-plus output on Peloton. Going fast to get your heart rate elevated, to be out of breath for a minute or two and pumping that oxygen to your brain, is a powerful benefit, especially for older adults,[5] and HIIT workouts have even been linked to improvements in mental well-being.[6]

One, perhaps obvious, correlation I've also noticed for myself is that intense exercise is accompanied by a dramatically increased water intake. And as we know, a well-hydrated brain is an especially alert and effective one.

If you really cannot find the energy to exercise or are recovering from an injury sidelining you from exercise, you might want to try a sauna or steam room! Saunas and steam rooms are backed by several studies that show a release of endorphins to improve your mood, and some studies show improvements in cognitive efficiencies as well.[7] ∎

If your brain had a battery level indicator during the day, what percentage would it show? What do you need it to show to accomplish what you're looking for?

There are 112 waking hours in a week (assumes eight hours asleep per day). Outside of your dedicated sleep time, how many hours do you spend in each state?

Percent	Activity	Hours
0%	Asleep or napping	_____ Hours
10%	Actively falling asleep or heavily inebriated	_____ Hours
20%	Post-all-nighter (without caffeine yet) tired	_____ Hours
30%	Less than five hours of sleep (or less than ~60 percent of your desired sleep level)	_____ Hours
40%	That post-big-meal malaise	_____ Hours
50%	Less than six hours of sleep (or less than 75 percent of your desired sleep level)	_____ Hours
60%	The 5:30 p.m. after sitting in an office all day feeling	_____ Hours
70%	Less than seven hours of sleep (or less than ~85 percent of your desired sleep level)	_____ Hours
80%	Morning cup of tea or coffee initial surge	_____ Hours
90%	Waking up from a nap or a rejuvenating full night's sleep	_____ Hours
100%	Fully alert feeling (that you can call upon daily)	_____ Hours
110%	Extreme clearheadedness from exercise, life moment, or flow state	_____ Hours

22. FIND ONE TO TWO HOURS PER DAY WHEN YOU CAN EXIST WITHOUT OTHERS' DISTRACTIONS

HABIT FORMATION

WE'VE ALL HEARD IT. Many famous folks swear by waking up early to accomplish their amazing feats. The 5:00 a.m. workouts, 4:00 a.m. bed-making, 5:30 a.m. sunrise meditations. That's all great and very inspiring, but what about for those of us who are bear and wolf sleep chronotypes?

In case you missed the memo on the sleep chronotypes, the wolf is the closest comparison to the more mainstream nighttime association of the owl. Putting it simply: Night timers, what are we supposed to do? Labor to become a lion? Become early birds seeking the coveted "worm"? Not necessarily.

The whole point of waking up early is to exist without distractions, to be able to think as clearly, be as productive, be as calm and collected as possible before you're swept off your feet. The good news is this whole experience also exists at night. At 10:30 p.m., 11:00 p.m., 11:30 p.m., 12:00 a.m.—whatever time your others go to bed, there's the time afterward. And don't let the early birds make you feel lesser than; there are some unique benefits to this approach as well. For starters, creativity is highest at night.

And if you're worried that dozing off on the couch may have cost you your window of creativity, fear not. A 2023 study by Harvard and MIT found that in the half-asleep state found between drifting and dreaming, scientifically called hypnagogia, we are our most creative.[8] They took the study a step further to show if you engaged in targeted dream incubation, where you're trying to focus on a particular topic before falling asleep, these literal dreamers were the most creative.

Additional studies showed that creativity was also at peak levels during mind-wandering—like when you're taking a shower, driving, or when your head is about to hit the pillow. We are free from our screens and daily social obligations, and our minds are unencumbered, available to come up with great ideas. Now, of course you can drive, shower, and perform any other activity during the day too, but this study from the *Journal of Environmental Psychology* showed that creativity was higher in dim lighting or darkness. Another point on the board for nighttime.[9]

While nighttime might be the right time for your creativity to take flight, it's not always easy. Nighttime can easily get away from you. After all, we are societally programmed to indulge in all entertainment…at night! The key is to set diligent limits around your entertainment. It's easy to call it a day like everyone else, but if you're an owl—understand it's not day-over for you—it's just hitting the pause button.

And once you have this completely clear time frame, don't waste it! Whether you're an early bird or a night owl—don't spend this precious time on activities you could do when you're not at your peak or on things you can accomplish while multitasking. For example, I almost always stay up later than my wife, so 11:15 p.m. to 1:00 a.m. is my time to maximize.

However, I often find myself cleaning dishes, feeding the fish or cat, taking out the garbage—a whole slew of tasks I shouldn't be doing between 11:15 p.m. and 12:15 a.m. Perhaps these are tasks that can be done as I turn my computer off and prepare for bed, but they are not tasks that should creep inside this crucial window. As we discussed earlier about keeping specific seats or spaces pure, keep your undistracted time pure. First, because how often are you really, truly, completely bereft of distractions? And secondly, you might not always have this time. A new job, new schedule, new family addition, and that time could be gone. Make the most of it while you have it. ∎

21. PUT UP YOUR "DO NOT DISTURB"—LITERALLY

PROTECT YOUR ALONE TIME

FOR YOUR OWN SAFETY, PLEASE STAND BEHIND THE YELLOW LINE.

@JUNHANCHIN

ONE OF THE hardest things to do is to find time when you're free from distractions. One thing that's even harder than finding the time is finding the space that's free from distractions.

That's why we need to manufacture these opportunities ourselves.

Pulling ourselves away from the action, telling the ones we love that we "need" to get back to work—there are many reasons why it's very hard to get away. And then worse yet, if you do manage to get away, you may have to battle the cognitive dissonance noise or the FOMO. This can overwhelm us so much that it leads us to go back earlier than desired, sometimes even immediately. If we do manage to stay in our separate space, we may end up texting or on social media staying in touch with those we just left. It's so difficult to get away and then be (quickly) productive after that.

That's why we need to *diligently* manufacture these opportunities ourselves.

And this process begins with the indications. Whether it's as direct as a literal sign or it's more coded like a closed door, flag, color-coded sticker, or some other indicator—there are many ways you can let people know, gently, that it's not a good time.

If the notification or signage is not universally recognized, provide them a very visible key so they cannot claim ignorance. An example of this would be the cracked door. There are many forms of a partially opened door, so let's begin with most people's interpretations of each:

- **Fully open door**: Free to come in
- **Half-open door**: Knock and enter
- **Mostly closed door**: Knock, ask if you can come in
- **Closed door**: Do not come in

Now these aren't universal, and depending upon who the potential infiltrators are, they might not care or might claim ignorance. This is where a key, like one you'd see on a map, is especially helpful. Without the key, the interruption and frustration will compound to set you further off course.

The next part of the process would be to provide the schedule. You can't be closed-door all day, as it's just not practical, and no matter how patient someone is, they aren't going to let that slide. People have questions and matters that need attention, so be fair in your scheduling. Try for no more than ninety minutes at a time without allowing someone the opportunity to talk to you, but manage your open windows by being specific about how long your breaks are. A good example of this is the pomodoro technique as it's specific on its work time and break time. Years back I had set up a texting notification system for my pomodoro techniques that notified people I was in the middle of a pomodoro and would respond at the end of my twenty-five-minute session during my next three-to-five-minute break.

Now that we have the indications, the key, and the schedule, the last item to set up is the facilitators. The facilitators are items that'll provide you with the headspace to work diligently without the extra noise of judgment, cognitive dissonance, FOMO, or anything else that gets in the (mental) way.

I discuss these more in other places throughout the book, but leveraging white noise (Practice 68) or music (Practice 50) are great ways to escape the half looking/half listening out for others and fully immerse yourself in your work. At the office this could be a desk fan; at a cubicle this could be your noise-canceling headphones; at home this could be the sound of a running shower or white noise machine.

If you're able to set clear indications, you'll create the space. A clear key and schedule will provide you the headspace. And the facilitators will create a "flow" space. ▪

20. WORK TOWARD YOUR LEGACY EVERY DAY

SINCE BIRTH I've had various digestive and stomach issues. It's made many moments in life difficult, from missed SAT tests to a cataclysmic engagement weekend; it's made the tough moments worse and put a damper on some of life's best moments too. These moments have amalgamated to give me seasons of constant uncertainty. Through years of tests, studies, and medications, it seemed it was never going to be solved. While I'm pleased to say having COVID-19, of all things, helped with a major breakthrough, it continues to be something I have to manage on a daily basis. This isn't being shared to gain sympathy or make you feel bad for me, but rather to share my story and what I consider my catalyst to hyperpresence and really a blessing from God.

As Ryan Holiday shares, "Blessings and burdens are not mutually exclusive," and I firmly believe blessing lies in many, perhaps even most, burdens.[10] For me, chronic severe pain and violent reactions have shown me that each moment in life is a blessing. Through the pain, I've had the good fortune of becoming supremely aware of time. This awareness has helped me turn off the societal autopilot, find my purpose ahead of schedule, and kick me into action. Without it, I don't think I'd be writing this book today. More than that, I don't think I'd spend my time each day thinking of ways to convey to others our need to find our God-given purpose, harness that energy and purpose, and work our asses off to make the world a better place. That better place is one that we all collectively want and all have inside us, but our potential contributions manifest in different, individual ways. It's like an 8.2-billion-piece puzzle, and we have to identify pieces, group them, and assemble.

All of this begins with a simple question: What's your purpose? It sounds like such a boring, common question, but if three different people asked you that question over as many days, would your answer be crisp, clear, and consistent? Sometimes it's the simplest questions that are the hardest and therefore require the most refinement.

Closely tied to that big question is another, slightly more inclusive question: What do you want to be remembered for? Perhaps you don't have your purpose crystallized just yet, but you do have your top skills, motivations, and characteristics solidified. The exploration and continuous reflection of these questions should be enough to fuel your actions each and every day.

Why exactly is that? Well, if you're doing it right, these two questions force us to operate with the end in mind: death.

We have only the one life, but when we're caught up consistently autopiloting it and doing everything in our power to avoid the topic of death, we end up thinking we're going to live forever. And I don't mean in some naive or delusional way that you, the reader, can disassociate yourself from. It's not something we are consciously doing; no, it's far scarier than that. It's a subconscious slide into oblivion.

Think about it: If you have no plan each day, no plan to take action, to improve, to learn, to move the chess piece forward, that means you think you have any time in the future to change course, not realizing you're losing each day that goes by. You're sacrificing a 100 percent guaranteed opportunity for a progressively smaller, sub-100-percent number in the future. And what is the future? *The future is simply an unknown number of upcoming, soon to take place, present moments.* And the past is a historical record of once-present moments immediately inscribed in pen, not pencil. There's no altering this record book. So if you can't change the past, and you can't rely on the future always being there, then what's your solution? ~~To do it~~ Today.

So let's review. By working toward our legacy every day, we have: (1) our day's (tackling) fuel and (2) our supreme, heightened awareness of presence.

For a third present or gift of this mindset, its "action above all else" mantra breaks the bounds of perfectionism.

I know many perfectionists, and you may be thinking, *Wow—folks obsessed with their work, the extremely hard work and self-critiquing talents that drive innovation and art.* Sometimes that is the case, yes, but more often than not—it's not. Perfectionists are so afraid to make a mistake they do little, or worse, *no* work. Being afraid something won't come out perfectly keeps you on your own self-imposed sideline waiting for a better time to start that, as we just discussed, may never come. It's why comics and writers have daily joke or word count minimums. Heck, as I write this at 11:41 p.m., tired and about to stop, I know it's not amazing but I'm getting it down on paper knowing I can revisit it another time to make it better or "nearly perfect" later. That's what editing is for after all. 😊

If you're someone who still likes the moniker of being a perfectionist, perfect the art of taking action. A perfectactionist.

Find a way every day to take a small step forward. Whatever the step is, it's forward. Don't obsess over the outcomes or markers of success either. At the end of the day, all we can control in life is our inputs. We can use feedback, advice, learnings from mistakes, research, and more to guide us on the most educated, thoughtful, and powerful inputs, but again they are only inputs. We do not control the outputs. I do not control the results of this very book in front of you; all I can do is control what I put into it. And as I type it, I'm channeling this action-orientation to guarantee this book sees the light of day. Whether it sells one thousand or one million copies after that is not up to me. The legacy I want to leave is as someone who tried *to do things in a thoughtful and thorough manner so others can thrive.* By simply publishing the book, I'm doing my part, my input, to solidify that legacy. ■

> For more on perfectionism and the studies showing the downsides of perfectionism, check out Chapter 3: The Imperfectionists in Adam Grant's *Hidden Potential*.

19. INSPIRATION–MOTIVATION–WILLPOWER–IDENTITY

I'M WPI. Drawing inspiration from Rocky to go work out is very good. Adopting Rocky as your role model for motivation is great. Reminding yourself that Rocky wouldn't quit when he gets tired is even better. Transforming the Italian Stallion into the Israeli Pony to make it your identity is the apex. Inspiration is one-off; identity is always. Inspiration defaults to *No, I can't.* Identity defaults to *Yes, I am.*

Once again, I-M-WP-I. No, I am not a physical college campus in Massachusetts; it's the mnemonic to remember the progression from inspiration to identity. This not-so-catchy acronym helps showcase the progression that comes with all the little things you "do" to build a person who is becoming, and to build an identity that's a legacy of who you have become.

Since we're going to talk about identity building more in coming sections, and motivation is simply the collection or continuation of inspiration(s), let's focus on the toughest definition of these four: willpower.

How exactly do you build willpower? Well, not only do you progress past motivation as shown in the example above, but you do so by addressing head-on the most difficult, least comfortable tasks. The ones that you really, really don't want to do. Those are the ones that build willpower. So, if you're looking to shortcut past the progression from inspiration to motivation to willpower and just jump straight to willpower, what can you do?

This is where those stereotypical, seemingly other-worldly people come into play with their extreme exercises. Yes, I'm talking about the ice baths. Yes, I'm talking about the cold showers. At least we got this far before I mentioned these departures from "everyday reality."

While most of the discussed benefits of cold plunging, ice bathing, or any other cold submersion are lackluster in their evidence, the mental well-being benefits are apparent.[11]

If you're like me and it would be medically unwise to try these techniques, here are some other ways you can consider building mental fortitude:

1. Fasting from food
2. Fasting from favorite items (akin to a devout Catholic's Lent)
3. Going to the gym when sleepy

4. Small, intentional exposure to a trigger or bad habit you're trying to break (quitting cold turkey also works)
5. Doing the most uncomfortable thing(s) you can think of (asking that person out on a date, facing a fear, etc.)
6. Pushing past your brain's first alarm system during a workout

These are just a few of the many ways you can climb the ladder to becoming the person you want to be each day instead of only recognizing yourself from time to time. ■

INSPIRATION   MOTIVATION   WILLPOWER   IDENTITY

ALEX DRIPCHAK &
@JUNINHNCHIN

REFLECTION

If you're not sure how much more impactful willpower and identity are over inspiration and motivation in your life, find a decision you struggle with often—perhaps it's deciding to either go to the gym or relax at home watching Netflix. Over the course of ten attempts, how many times would inspiration lead you to getting to your desired, productive choice? How many times for motivation? Now let's contrast these hypotheticals to actuals.

Take another 50/50 choice scenario you're more effective at and ask yourself, *How many times can I call upon a dose of willpower?* Lastly, take something you feel strongly about. Perhaps it's being a (insert sports team here) fan. Maybe it's being a reader. A runner. A cook. If you made a choice between something that's a part of your identity versus something that isn't, how many times out of ten does identity win? This progressively higher buildup articulates the point that willpower and identity are far more reliable than inspiration and motivation.

18. TRANSFORM ACTIONS INTO IDENTITIES

FOR EXTRA EFFECT, here's another way of performing Practice 19.

It isn't "I read"; it's "we are readers." It isn't "I like to run"; it's "we are runners."

Turning the focus from the action (reading) to the subject (reader) is powerful. It's your own personal endorsement, your testimony of your life and what you enjoy doing. It's what you prioritize and what you will be remembered by. It's a core part of your identity.

As you can see, I've taken Practice 19 a step further by skipping from "I" to "we." Finding a community to associate yourself with is a powerful, extra boost on your identity-building habit journey. Its power is derived not only from its network of built-in accountability partners and relationships with high achievers, but also from the fact that having a community turns your journey from one of an individual plight and individual habit enforcement to a habit formation journey of collective support and progression. This change is a powerful way to achieve more.

Now there's one big pitfall here that I have seen and been guilty of: subscribing to the label without earning it quite yet. You should turn your desired, positive actions into an identity only once it has become a habit. As you develop the habit, you can start by saying, "I'm aspiring to become," "I am working toward becoming," or, for later stages, "I am becoming a _____."

Like the caterpillar example we discussed earlier, the four stages of transformation here could be: *I'm aspiring to become* a writer. *I'm working toward becoming* a writer. *I am becoming* a writer. *I am* a writer.

"I am" is the most powerful phrase in the English language; respect its power and use it only once you can confidently say it. If you can say it wholeheartedly with the kind of assurance and poise it deserves, without pause, without trying to convince yourself, without guilt—you know you've made the label.

Once you're established, remove "becoming" or any words similar to it.

Another caution: For any negative actions, don't use "I am." Don't say, "I'm not worthy," "I'm ashamed," or "I am terrible." None of those. If you feel down or doubting after a slipup, say that. *Feel.* "I feel ashamed." "I felt dumb saying." "I feel like I could have done better."

You can also say "I noticed" or "I found": "I noticed I didn't engage well with so-and-so" or "I found myself challenged by that." Remove identity from your words and replace it with a phrase that articulates it as, or treats it as, a one-off instance.

Disassociate identity from anything negative, and replace it with instance. One time you felt this way. You have 1,000 times where you felt capable and powerful. One time? One measly time? That's not even a percent. You know what it is? It's insignificant. It's forgettable. It's not worth being concerned about. It's not *it's* anymore. *It's* implies present. It is. You know what it is? It *was*. It was a concern, and it no longer exists. It was. ◼

17. WRITE AND SIGN YOUR OWN HABIT CONTRACT

ANY GOOD HABIT contract should follow three steps:

1. Make it written.
2. Make it known.
3. Make it public.

If you are looking for a good standard habit contract, I would advise you to check out Jim Kwik's book *Limitless*, but a habit contract doesn't have to be restricted to our mind's depiction of the word "contract." It doesn't have to be a physical piece of paper outlined in contractual language. No, it can be much more, or less, than that. For me, it takes the form of Instagram posts.

Each year I post publicly what I'm setting out to accomplish by the end of the year. To ensure it's something I'm in control of, it's an input I have say over. On the post I further detail my goals and why they're important to me to ensure maximal commitment. While helpful, there are limitations to this approach. By having it online I unfortunately do not have the satisfaction of an official paper document, and I also miss out on the act of signing a contract. An agreement is only valid once it's been signed. Endorsed. Executed. Initialed. Stamped. However you say it, it should have some personal endorsement next to it so it goes beyond just saying it to the next level of: I forever said this, it's a law as immutable as gravity, a mark that will stand the test of time.

To combine the best of both worlds, next year I'll have to sign the agreement and then post a picture of it online. Written, known, public—check all three off the list.

Now ask yourself, what is so important to me that I can break my comfort zone, enlist accountability partners, tell the world about it, and tie it all together by putting my forever mark on? That's the subject of your new contract. ■

16. MAKE YOUR GOALS KNOWN TO MANY

CLOSELY TIED TO Practice 17, this section takes the habit contract and propels it further. Tell your goals to others. Many of them. And be judicious about who you tell. You want to tell not only those who listen closely (perhaps your parents), but also those who can serve as accountability partners (maybe your parents, but maybe not). Focus on the goals you can control and make them SMART goals so there are clearly defined times and metrics to check in on these goals later.

> ## ACTIVE RECALL QUIZ
>
> What does SMART stand for in relation to setting SMART goals? Bonus points: What does SMARTPURECLEAR stand for?

The principle here of "I said I was going to do it, so I'm going to do it" is hard at work. Now some of you may counter with, "I don't need to tell others. If I tell myself I'm going to do it, I'm going to do it." While this is true, the difference is if you don't follow through, your reputation won't be stained or tarnished. There would be no log against your integrity or commitment. If you don't do it, no matter how small, insignificant, downright miniscule it is, it would still be filed in someone's mind as: "Well they don't do every single thing they say they are going to do." This is totally fine, as nobody is perfect, but wouldn't you rather not have any questions of your commitment, integrity, trustworthiness, or work ethic?

What you can control—your inputs—make that public. Dale Carnegie has a likeability principle that instructs to give people a fine reputation to live up to, and you should do the same for yourself; give yourself a reputation to uphold, and build the reputation of someone who keeps their word.[12] If you're already doing it privately, consider finding ways to make some of these commitments public; it's a win for your reputation and for others to get to know you. ∎

15. GET YOUR THIRTY-PLUS MINUTES OF EXERCISE, FOUR TIMES PER WEEK

ENERGY CULTIVATION

Sometimes it's the simple things that are the most important. Not only because they're commonly expressed, but because their simplicity makes them easily forgettable. It's nothing new and catchy, and for that reason we often put the simple things on the back burner in favor of searching for the next groundbreaking idea. However, the old and simple things are absolutely crucial to get right. Like Stephen Covey says in *The 7 Habits of Highly Effective People*, spending two hours each week to improve the other 166 is a no-brainer. To all those who say they don't have the time, Covey offers some commentary: "Most of us think we don't have enough time to exercise. What a distorted paradigm! We don't have time not to."[13]

Dr. Julie Smith adds in her book *Why Has Nobody Told Me This Before?* that exercise leads to higher circulating levels of dopamine as well as more available dopamine receptors in the brain. This means exercise increases your capacity for pleasure in everyday life. Finding exercise you enjoy not only offers you joy during and after exercise, but also "increases your sensitivity to find joy in all the other aspects of your life."[14] Further research shows that doing anything more than your usual amount of movement will help boost your willpower.

So, in summary: Exercise improves your sleep and boosts your productivity, ability to find joy, and willpower. It's such a powerful practice that I might have to bump this up from Practice 15.

For me to maximize my day, I find exercise sometime between 3:00 and 5:30 p.m. to be most effective. It's said that most of us hit our wall or lull, due to our circadian rhythm, anywhere from 2:00 to 4:00 p.m.,[15] and for me the lull usually comes in the latter part of that window. In addition to breaking the afternoon slump, I often need to be at peak energy level from 4:00 to 9:00 p.m., so a workout midday gets me that energy boost while allowing me to come down from peak levels to get to bed by my 12:45 a.m. bedtime goal. If you have the flexibility to exercise at the peak times for your day's performance, I highly recommend it. If you don't have flexibility, try to combat the afternoon slump by taking a walk outside, as sunlight can be a nice way to combat the melatonin production of your circadian rhythm that seems to lull most of us to "sleep" in the mid to late afternoon.

Now that we're on the topic of sleep, and timetables to do so, you want to be cognizant of how your body responds to exercise. Studies vary on how far in advance of bedtime to stop exercise, but the minimum recommendation I found was one hour, and most reports advocated for closer to three hours or more in advance. This Harvard study found that those who tried to go to bed within one hour of finishing physical exercise struggled to fall asleep.[16] Get your exercise in but try to avoid those very late nights at the gym. ∎

14. FIND YOUR WORKING RHYTHM

THERE ARE THREE widely accepted models of time management for work. The most widely known, and likely practiced, is the pomodoro technique. The pomodoro technique proposes that for every twenty-five to thirty minutes of work, you take a three- to five-minute break. This is most commonly seen as twenty-five minutes on, five minutes off.

The next most common rhythm would be the 52/17 model from the app DeskTime, made famous by its inclusion in Daniel Pink's book *When*. This study showed that the app's top performers averaged fifty-two minutes of deep work immediately followed by a break of seventeen minutes.[17] If this rhythm looks familiar, it's for good reason—it's the one that most closely follows our typical hour-long work meetings or, for a more ingrained time frame, the common fifty minute, three-times-per-week college course.

The final working rhythm is the 10/1 model put forth by neuroscientist Earl Miller, and as its name would suggest, it's for quicker sprints of ten minutes working and a single one-minute break.[18]

Whether it's the 25/5 of pomodoro, the 10/1 methodology studied by Miller, or the 52/17 study by DeskTime, find your working rhythm and stick to it. The average worker is distracted every three minutes—don't let that be you.

You will likely find that depending on the task, each of these is helpful. For tasks that are your most difficult to commit to mentally and do not require a flow state for strong results, maybe try the ten minutes on, one minute off methodology. The breaks are short and are a quick jolt, but given their spacing, they're always just a few minutes away and make any task, no matter how laborious, just manageable enough.

Personally I like the pomodoro for about 75 percent of tasks, and the remaining 25 percent are split almost evenly between the 10/1 for more laborious or less interesting tasks to keep me on pace and the 52/17 (or even longer rhythms) for more involved tasks like creating a presentation deck or writing this book (tasks that benefit from a flow state).

What I love about the 25/5 pomodoro technique is it takes your days and chunks them into half hours. It's simple, memorable, and readily achievable.

Moreover, it takes advantage of recency and latency—which tells us that roughly the first twelve minutes and last twelve minutes of what was learned/

comprehended is what we engage with and remember most. So, twenty-five minutes on minimizes that trough of inattention and lack of memory capability to a single solitary minute. Now you'll realize the total break time is longer than three 10/1 method cycles, but sometimes it's easier to knock out what's waiting for you if your break is five minutes rather than just one minute. An insufficient break may cause you to delay your working rhythm and therefore devalue adherence to the schedule, or it'll occupy headspace while you try and get back on task. Either way, the 10/1 methodology is risky to use as your primary structure. Whether it's a structure detailed here or one you create yourself, find your rhythm and try to spend at least 50 percent of your working day in that rhythm. ■

13. LET GO OF THE PAST; MINIMIZE THE PRESSURES OF THE FUTURE AND SEIZE THE NOW

"Yesterday is history, tomorrow is a mystery, and today is a gift. That is why it's called the present."

—BILL KEANE

TODAY

@JUNHANCHIN

YESTERDAY   **TOMORROW**

IF YOU RECEIVED your utilization report at the end of each day, would you be happy with what it said?

Or to take a step back, would you even know what it would say?

Well, let's see. What time did you wake up today? _____

Now, take what time it is now and subtract it from the time you woke up.

_____

Of that time you've been up, what have you done? Could you account for every hour? Every half hour? Every ten minutes? How about close to every minute?

It's a tall task, but the point gets us to recognize just how time blind we are. We often operate on a daily basis when we want to be thinking on an hourly basis, or at peak times we're on an hourly basis when we want to be on a minutes basis.

As Ryan Holiday reminds us, every minute is yours to use.

It's a powerful recalibration, and just like earlier when we explored how any random day can be a great day of breakthrough, not just January 1, any minute of the day can be that moment of breakthrough.

So what is it that keeps us from using minutes, or at least hours, as a frame of reference?

Time. If I were to ask you what percentage of your time you spend living in the past, present, and future, what would you say? I think you might quickly realize just how much the past and future can be reducing our lives.

The only time that we ever exist in is the present. If you look at 95-plus percent of circumstances, there's nothing wrong with the now. We often hinder ourselves ruminating over past mistakes, embarrassments, heartbreaks, and disappointments, or we're too busy worrying about future events that haven't occurred yet. Worse, we might sometimes combine these two forces when thinking, *What if during tomorrow's presentation my computer dies like it did ten years ago during that client meeting at ABC company?*

When you're able to minimize the past and future, you reduce so much noise in your mind and attain a heightened sense of presence, being, feeling, doing. It's almost an out-of-body experience showing us a level of attunement we never knew possible.

If these very meta, very deep revelations don't move you toward hyper-presence, perhaps something more concrete will help:

On average we get 29,585 days in life.

From birth until eighteen years old we are dependent on others. At sixty-five we are expected to retire, and for some this means we contribute less to the world.

That leaves ages eighteen to sixty-four for us to maximize. For those who opt for college, eighteen becomes twenty-two before we're able to contribute as fully. For some, retirement is earlier at age sixty. So now we're looking at optimizing twenty-two to sixty. Eighty-one years is now all of a sudden down to thirty-eight. That means 29,585 days has, in two lines of text, become 13,880 days. We all recognize life is short, but it just got a lot shorter.

Now for those who say, "Wow! I have over ten thousand days—that means any single day is only .01 of a percent. In other words, I've got one hundred days until I even hit 1 percent of my time—what a relief!" If thinking of life as eighty-one years was the first problem, the second, and perhaps more dangerous, problem is believing every single day is currently being maximized, or even utilized.

Of your last month, how many days would you say you were very proud of your output, your contributions to others, and your impact? Let's assume you said one per week—or four per month. That's 1,850 days or just over five years. Let's say you work a job you describe as "it pays the bills." In your after-hours you watch a lot of TV, tend to your chores and errands, and therefore only feel confident in saying you contribute one day per month to building a legacy you're proud of. This drop to a single monthly contribution means you're down to a total of 462 days or 1.26 years of contribution. Wow. Let that settle in for a moment. If you're passively pursuing that dream job, that dream date, or that dream lifestyle, you're shortchanging yourself out of a minimum potential 13,418 days and only truly living 3.3 percent of the time. Not to mention you're putting a *lot* of pressure on those 462 days to pan out, to be fruitful, to be productive, to be…enough.

Andrew Sachs is credited with the powerful maxim: Everyone dies but not everyone lives. I'd like to reframe this quote as everyone dies enough but not everyone lives enough. One day per month means you're really "living" just over 3 percent of the time.

So to add perhaps an even more powerful quote and wish for you upon reading this passage, let's go to eighteenth-century essayist and poet Jonathan Swift for a profound blessing of the utmost abundance:

May you live all the days of your life. (Or at least more than half.) ◾

12. PLAY OUT YOUR FLY ON THE WALL SCENARIO: WHAT DO THEY SAY? WHAT SHOULD THEY SAY?

AKIN TO A deathbed meditation, this section could be called Leading a Legacy-Leaving Living (just came up with it now but I'm going to use it). In legacy-leaving living, or LLL for short, you switch the focus from your deathbed or very old age to this present moment and ask:

If I were a fly on the wall behind closed doors with the people who matter most in my life's well-being and they were asked, "What's your no bones about it, very transparent view of (*your name here*)? What are they all about? How would you describe them to others? Would you recommend someone be friends with them? Hire them? Take their advice?"

If you're answering honestly, what would they say?

Now, what *should* they say?

How big is that gap, and are you comfortable with that gap? To put it another way, if you died today (God forbid) would you regret that gap, that delta between would and should? What can you do now that's inside your control, your inputs, that can help close that gap?

Perhaps there is no gap. Not because you're living a completely fulfilling life but because you haven't been clear on how you want to be remembered. Either your words, actions, or both haven't made that abundantly clear. If this is your concern, how can you be more intentional in your legacy-leaving living? You hear it all the time—be more intentional—and oftentimes our reaction is, "Gee, thanks for the amazing advice" with a not-so-subtle dose of sarcasm administered. However, when it comes to a perceived image gap, intentionality is the cure.

If you set out each day focused on the legacy you're going to leave and you show people just that—well then that's just the natural course of observation. Through observation and its osmosis, they will learn how you want to be remembered, and coming back to this on even a quarterly basis gives you four more times—for however many more years you'll be on this earth—than most.

Deathbed, assisted living facility, homebound, retirement, kid's college graduation—those are the five times I can think of when I hear people talk most about their intentional legacy. The problem with this approach? Well, for starters, three of these times the person isn't seeing enough people to cast out their intentions wide enough and, like it or not, by this stage of life, a legacy has already been written! The book has been written, we're editing the conclusion stage, and now, just now, you finally thought about the first chapter? The typewriter of life has been hidden away stamping its immutable biography in silence. This sad realization means most people are left with just two potentially course-adjusting legacy-leaving living self-reflections, and unfortunately for them, both time frames are when people are often in their fifties and sixties with most of their impact, and the majority of their years, behind them.

Contrast that to someone who does this legacy-leaving living exercise four times per year beginning at age thirty. This person has eighty more check-ins with themselves before the standard person even thinks of moment one.

For me, my legacy-leaving living is in what I call the Life Checkup that I've copied here. The three buckets are:

1. How am I feeling?
2. How well am I doing?
3. Who am I becoming? (Or for easier grading: Do I like who I'm becoming?)

On a 1 to 10 scale, where 1 is terrible, 10 is fantastic, and 5 is neither good nor bad, how would you score yourself? ▪

Feeling	Doing	Becoming
Energy:	Job:	Passions:
Attitude:	Career:	Aspirations:
Happiness:	Finances:	Growth:
Inner peace:	Health:	Purpose:
Fulfillment:	Friends:	Legacy:
	Family:	Spirituality:
	Love life:	

11. ARRANGE YOUR DAY THE NIGHT BEFORE

MOST OF OUR DAYS are spent reacting to the demands of others, autopiloting, scrolling, and entertaining ourselves.

It's a sad truth we must face.

Fortunately there's a great and simple antidote: Write down what you want to accomplish the next day.

This simple practice is especially beneficial if you're someone tracking many areas of life. Considering most reports show 36 to 54 percent of Americans have two or more jobs/side hustles, I imagine a great deal of you are balancing very full, diversified days.

Some of you may see this practice as an organizational benefit but not necessarily a productivity benefit. While it may not immediately look like a productivity enhancer, it has latent value. When you have things mapped out, you move more quickly from task to task. You're not constantly left wondering, *What should I do next?* or, more dangerously, *What do I want to do now?*

If you're moving from task to task without a plan, there's no denominator. You don't know what task you accomplished out of the total, and you're treating each task like it could be the last of the day. However, when you set an accurate list of to-dos the night before, you know how much more you have to get done and therefore the downtime, break time, or transition time is shortened.

Beyond the list-making of aspirational accomplishments, arranging your day the night before could be something as simple as:

1. Clearing off your desk and decluttering your environment to hit the ground running the next morning
2. Calendaring what tasks you will dedicate time for throughout the day
3. Writing down the items that'll have the greatest impact on your personal and professional success that day

Now I specify "night before" opposed to "morning of" because personally I've noticed the days I wake up earlier, I jump right into action more so than plan out my day. You could do whatever works best for you, but I would encourage even the morning birds to try preparing the night before. There's something psychological about feeling pride in having tomorrow mapped out, and just like practice or rehearsal makes us more confident, arranging and organizing a day the night before provides a level of reassurance that I find helps me sleep better too.

Overall, the more numerous and varied the tasks you have for the following day, the more you need to prioritize arranging your day the night before. Block off anywhere from thirty to sixty minutes to do this planning. If that sounds like a lot, use the untapped brain power, or rather unfocused brain power, during your evening commute, time preparing dinner, or that before-bed shower to start thinking of what you can outline or add to your night-before arrangement. ◾

10. KEEP A POSITIVE PEER GROUP

WE'VE ALL HEARD the famous theory that we are the average of the five people we are closest to. While I didn't find any studies to delve into the matter, conceptually it makes sense. And while you may not look at your five biggest time spender-with-ers and think, *I fit right smack in the middle(!)*, you may recognize the concept's guidance to surround ourselves with a strong support system.

Whether we like it or not, for better or worse, we all fall victim to proximity comparison at some time or another. Perhaps you run circles around your friends, or you feel your friends are the ones etching the sphere around you. Point being, it's easy to artificially extrapolate the world based on the limited number of people whose near-daily moves we know.

I've already warned against how negativity and complaining are some of the biggest time sucks and critical thinking drains, but here's a new potential concern: friends who are too positive.

We all know Negative Nancy, but are we as keenly aware of Head in the Clouds Hailey or Out of Touch Oscar? This could be the friend or family member who thinks you are so far ahead of everyone else and therefore encourages the wrong, or unrealistic, actions.

Most of my life I've heard "You're always working so hard! You should take a break or just relax with us." People were so keen to fan the flames either because they thought they were being the helpful firefighter or they were the coy iceberg afraid that being too close to the fire would force them to change state. Whichever the reason, they didn't realize they were putting out the fire as opposed to figuring out ways to help stoke it. So, your friends should certainly be positive, but they should more importantly be:

- Helpful
- Inspirational
- Realistic

Basically they should be HIR.

No matter how well you're doing at these one hundred performance optimization exercises, it's tough to truly thrive if you're being held back—or worse, held down—by those closest to you. So, to shift the focus from my intentionally misleading section title, *instead of looking for positivity, look for positive influence.*

Ask yourself: *Does this person make me a better person? Do they support the identity I want to have? Better yet, do they aid or streamline that progression?* A word of caution for this exercise: Treat this as an opt-in, not an opt-out, exercise. This means that not only the nos, but also the neutrals, should be left off your list. While it's tempting to see the good in folks, you should have an honest assessment that counts only those who are actively, truly helping or trying to help you.

Treating this as an opt-out exercise keeps too many passives in your inner circle and only causes more headaches, especially from a time management perspective. Treating this as an opt-in exercise makes you astutely aware of who helps you most, and helps you appreciate and reciprocate to those folks. Unfortunately, by and large, people don't go out of their way unless they really care, so be thankful for those few and be one of those few in return. This satisfies the H in HIR.

Now for the I—inspirational. Jay Shetty recommends spending at least 75 percent of your time with people who inspire you rather than bring you down.[19] Ideally someone is helpful and inspirational, but that borders on unicorn-frolicking. You want to find those who are truly exceptional in one of the areas and are keen to be a part of your circle.

Now, if your current community exists in a space completely separate from your own and you're having trouble finding this group of inspirational people to be in your circle, go where you cultivate your energy source (e.g., a gym, church) or go where people are growing, like a workshop, conference, language learning class, sport practice, club, volunteer activity, spiritual retreat, etc. Those acutely focused on growth are likely to be inspiring.

Lastly, we have realistic. Everyone has the hype and/or noncombative friends. I'd estimate noncombatives make up 90 percent of people's friends. Conversely, you'll also see a few percent of people who like to complain about everything, and their first comment is something negative or that something could have been done better. For identifying the realistic, ask yourself, *Who are the master compliment-sandwich makers—those who recognize my most differentiated strengths yet pinpoint the gap, the weakness, the feedback I need to hear?* That's the feedback that will elevate you to the next level. These are the people you want in your circle as well.

So your five closest people? Well hopefully Mom and Dad satisfy two of these three traits, but it's not probable, which means your spouse, best friend, and business partner or closest colleague should be at least one of these three. Don't aim for a unicorn who has all three HIR traits; instead seek to round out your five with a role player for each. After all, the Dream Team didn't have five shooting guards. In order to operate at peak levels, everyone has a role to play; who's playing your roles of HIR? And better yet, which people are you being H, I, or R to? ■

WHO IS HELPFUL, INSPIRATIONAL, AND REALISTIC TO YOU?

Helpful	Inspirational	Realistic

WHO ARE YOU HELPFUL, INSPIRATIONAL, AND REALISTIC TO?

Helpful	Inspirational	Realistic

9. CREATE TIME BY COMBINING

TIME MANAGEMENT

IF I TOLD YOU I read twenty-three books in 2022—you would probably say, "OK that's cool and all but not that impressive." If I said I read every single page of each of those books, you'd probably say that's good commitment but still not that impressive. But how about if I said I did it without dedicating a single moment to reading? Would that at least get an eyebrow raise?

It typically does, and here's what I mean by it: I didn't dedicate any time in my schedule for reading. Instead it was done in the doctor's office waiting room, walking to and from the office, waiting on the subway, taking a bath—even something as short as riding the elevator. This showed me that each day we lose so much time just by waiting, avoiding, sitting, simply because it's not visible time loss.

While most things we cannot effectively multitask, there are many things we do separately that could be combined, like the age-old adage: We can both walk and chew gum. For me, it's working while walking on the treadmill. Reading while commuting. Responding to texts or overdue emails via phone call while traveling.

Whenever I tell people I took a run or walk during a listen-in-only call they respond with, "I should have done that! Or at least gone outside!" I hear the genuine frustration in their voice. Life is busy enough, and here was a golden opportunity missed!

We are conditioned to associate working with sitting, stationary with necessary. Break this societal construct. For many reasons it's working to your detriment—physically and mentally we perform better when in motion. As the body moves, the brain grooves.

Ask yourself: *Do I find myself sedentary for certain tasks? How could I help break that conformity? What are the golden opportunities I could be capitalizing on but I'm missing due to routine, optics, or pure societal construct?*

The one I constantly kick myself for is sitting inside while catching up on the phone with my parents. I could have been outside getting some sun, going for a walk, driving to a destination, or any other productive, beneficial activity. A habit stack here could work wonders. For example, for every time I call my parents, I'm going to walk three thousand steps. This is productive, makes time go by quickly, and is time-bound to prevent conversations from running longer than expected.

I cannot underscore the importance of intentionality when it comes to spending your time. To help build daily awareness and get the productivity juices flowing, I created the following list to show how anyone could find literal days of unoccupied thinking, or doing, opportunities. Now, I wouldn't recommend anyone fill all these times with productive activities because, after all, you need some time to daydream in order to problem solve, think creatively, or simply take a break! Or other times you want to just think about family, friends, love, hobbies, sports—the myriad of topics that life needs for balance. ■

So where do we strike that balance; what is the golden ratio? Anecdotally, it'll vary for each person, but I'd suggest capitalizing on anywhere from 20 to 60 percent of your unoccupied free time opportunities. Imagine what you could accomplish with just a 20 percent reappropriation of free time? Or even half that; can you commit to reallocating 10 percent of your unoccupied free time to doing something productive? How about an extra five days a year to produce something that you'll be proud of? Perhaps this is the time that leads to your big breakthrough at work? A patent? A promotion? A book deal? A news article? A groundbreaking innovation? A cure? You never know. The time for great ideas is everywhere. ■

Time Creators
When Is Your Mind Free?

Magnitude of Impact (MOI)

7

Additions

Daily (x365)

1. Elevator Ride: 30sec ×6
2. Subway Ride: 15min ×2
3. Subway Platform: 3min ×2
4. Walk to Work: 10min ×2
5. Bathroom: 5min
6. Shower: 10min
7. Brushing Teeth: 1min
8. Gym: 30min

105 Minutes/Day = 40 Waking Days/Year

Boosters

Weekly (x52)

1. Drive to Church: 10min ×2
2. Drive to Dinner: 15min ×2
3. Drive to Errands: 10min ×2
4. Laundy: 60min
5. Supermarket: 45min

175 Minutes/Week = 9.5 Waking Days/Year

Added Value

Monthly (x12)

1. Playing Golf: 90min
2. Extended Drive: 90min
3. Run/Hike/Bike: 60min
4. Suntanning: 90min

330 Minutes/Month = 4 Waking Days/Year

Bonus

Quarterly (x4)

1. Vacation: 60min ×3
2. Beach: 45min ×2
3. Doctor's Office: 15min
4. DMV/Other Waiting Area: 30min
5. Flight: 120min ×2

555 Minutes/Quarter = 2.3 Waking Days/Year

What could you accomplish with an extra 56 days/year?

8. GET THE SLEEP YOU NEED

ENERGY CULTIVATION

LIKE PRACTICE 36, this may be one where I get some eye rolls. And while I'll admit it's a simple one, it's important to note that there are few things in life that increase your productivity more than sleeping well, and there are even fewer things that can derail you faster and further off course than a lack of sleep.

With 40 percent of America chronically sleep deprived, here are some tips to help make this practice achievable:[20]

1. No screen time or bright lights at least thirty minutes before bed. You're telling your body to rise by showing it light. To help ensure you keep this principle actionable, shower, read, or write a list of to-dos or thoughts before you go to bed.
   a. The pro tip here would be to get in the habit of low or dim lighting two hours before bed to more gently prepare yourself for sleep.

2. Sleep with your phone more than three feet away from you. Blue light emission keeps you up and prevents restful sleep.

3. Consider taking half doses of melatonin. Recommendation is .5 mg, but I personally need 1.5 mg—be careful as over-the-counter serving size usually recommends two gummies for 5 mgs, almost ten times the therapeutic dose.

4. Keep your room cool! Your body needs to cool its core temperature to fall asleep, and this is a hack to get it to do so faster. Experts say for the best-quality sleep you should keep your room between 60 and 68 degrees Fahrenheit,[21] with Sleep Foundation reporting a narrower range of 65–68 degrees.[22] Temperatures above 75 or below 54 can disrupt sleep. Another way to cool your core temperature is in your presleep routine: Take a warm bath! If you struggle to get tired at night and have already tried low lighting, reduced screen time, and no caffeine or exercise within six hours of bedtime, try a warm

room—above 75 degrees—to make you tired enough to go to bed. This works best if you have two zones for air conditioning, as to stay asleep you want to have a cool room, and 75 degrees actively works against sleep quality.

5. Get blue-light-reducing covers for your phone and your computer. Invest in the battle against overexposure of blue light! It strains your eyes, keeps you awake, and reduces the quality of your sleep. Stop letting it get in the way.

6. Don't concentrate on sleep—concentrate on relaxation. Hyperfocusing on how you need to go to sleep produces anxiety, and it's a dangerous cycle of rumination. Instead, focus on what helps you relax and let your body do the rest. If rumination—or what Dr. Romie Mushtaq calls the Busy Brain in her book *The Busy Brain Cure*—still persists, make sure you're going to sleep when you're sufficiently tired, not just because someone else went to sleep, you want to/have to go to bed early, or any other forced, contrived reason that puts your misled head in bed ahead of sched(ule).[23] If you still can't sleep, get out of bed and do some deep breathing or meditation in another room. Or try reading in a lowly lit room with a reading light.

For the full list of tips on how to be best prepared to battle this ultimate "energy guzzler," review the following graphic. If you need one extra push to take this review seriously, consider this: *The Happiness Project* author, and creator of the above-mentioned energy guzzler terminology, Gretchen Rubin shares that a lack of sleep weakens memory and metabolism.[24] So, if you won't do it as a boost to your productivity, make the checklist that follows a part of your routine for the sake of preserving your memory and metabolism. ■

2–9 Hours in Advance

- ☑ Plan around tomorrow's calendar
- ☐ Avoid caffeine (3–9)
- ☐ Finish exercise (3–9)
- ☐ Eat a banana
- ☐ Finish food (2–4)
- ☐ Low light/candlelight (1–3)

0–2 Hours Before Bed

- ☑ Have a calming tea/patch
- ☐ Stop screen time (30–90min)
- ☐ Cool down bedroom
- ☐ Keep a worry list bedside
- ☐ Therapeutic dose of melatonin
- ☐ Place electronics out of reach
- ☐ Take a warm bath
- ☐ Read

After Eye Shut and Next Morning

- ☑ Concentrate on relaxation
- ☐ Use a progressive sound alarm
- ☐ Get up and set intentions
- ☐ Get outside (30min)
- ☐ Track your sleep
- ☐ Maintain your routine with sleep profile
- ☐ Avoid your bed(room)
- ☐ Avoid napping

7. DON'T LET TIREDNESS TAKE OVER

IN A WEIRD WAY, being tired can be attractive, an unusual enticement, like Odysseus's Sirens song: Something you know isn't real but are drawn to. I guess a modern, lighter analogy could be that feeling of hope when you see a $100 bill on the ground. You're very sure it's not real, yet you bend down to check and end up falling for someone's ruse. Being, or labeling yourself as, tired is similarly tricky. Sometimes your body is calling for rest, but often feeling down, uninspired, stagnant, or just plain bored gets misappropriated as "tired." Next time you feel "tired," dig deeper; most of the time, you'll do better to cultivate energy than call it a day.

If you need some quick ways to help squash tiredness and an ice bath or an ice-cold shower aren't what you want to hear, try these three basics first.

Hydrate

A lack of fluids can cause your heart to pump faster to supply oxygen to your body, making it more difficult to get a consistent flow of oxygen to your brain.

Even mild dehydration can cause reductions in concentration, memory, and reaction time.[25] So to be physically firing at your best, first make sure you're hydrated.

Two other things you're more likely to avoid when properly hydrated that could sideline your productivity? Digestion issues and headaches. No matter how good your music playlist, primed environment, and focus are, if you're hit by significant medical issues, you'll experience reductions in productivity. This is one I know all too well, unfortunately.

Get Outside

Spending time outside has many benefits that we've already covered, so here's a quick recap.

Serotonin regulation from sunlight helps raise energy and helps keep us calm and focused. Being outside encourages better breathing. Getting outdoors provides rejuvenation and helps us recharge and build problem-solving abilities.

Maybe it's to another person or perhaps, to avoid distraction, it's just talking out loud to yourself. Yes, talking to yourself—that often taboo thing to discuss and seldom admit is beneficial.[26]

So before you succumb to tiredness or have to find the time to get caffeine or a workout in, try this three-part triage: HOT—Hydration, Outdoors, Talking.

If you notice some improvements and don't have the opportunity to call upon the proverbial big guns of energy cultivation, here are a few more ideas to try after checking your HOT status.

Three coincidental additional remedies to HOT all involve cold. Cold helps activate adrenaline to give you a quick jolt of energy.[27] So if HOT doesn't do the trick, try splashing your face with cold water, drinking a very cold glass of water, or rubbing an ice cube on your wrist.

For some odd, helpful techniques, you can try a pull of your hair (to get blood flowing to your head) or the hotly contested inversion therapy, a.k.a. hanging/lying upside down. Provided it's for sixty seconds or less, I'm personally on team upside down, but first consult with your doctor, especially if you have increased risk factors.

If none of these are your cup of tea per se, then you may want to try a different cup: peppermint tea. The aroma of peppermint, and peppermint oil, has menthol properties, and various studies have tied it to enhancements in memory, processing speed, and alertness.[28]

6. FOR GOOD HABITS, REDUCE FRICTION. FOR BAD, ADD.

HABIT FORMATION

James Clear's *Atomic Habits* teaches us this powerful lesson: Anything you want to do, make it easier to do.[29] And conversely, anything you want to do less of, or remove altogether, insert steps to make it more difficult. You can make running easier by putting your running shoes next to your front door. This way it's physically impossible to leave without seeing them and removing them from the path of the doorway. You can make watching TV more difficult by taking the batteries out of the remote.

The concept teaches us about visibility, clarity, satisfaction, and difficulty. For a more complete guide, see the following examples:

Good habit to encourage: Exercise

1. Put your shoes by the door.
2. Work out with someone else.
3. Go the same time each scheduled day.
4. Have a friend you only see at the gym.

Bad habit to reduce or eliminate: TV

1. Turn it off.
   a. Maybe most folks do this so it sounds silly, but growing up in my house, the TV was always on. Volume might have been low or off, but the screen was always on. Sure, I learned some things about the stock market through osmosis, but 97 percent of the time, the distractions were not beneficial. If you're in the habit of leaving the TV on, step one is muting it. Step two is turning it off. Be intentional about TV time; otherwise, everything else in your day will suffer. Ninety-nine percent of the programs wouldn't appeal to us enough to make us turn on the TV, but they keep our interest when the TV is already on. And since no action is needed (all you have to do is watch) we end up getting distracted. Turn one hundred-plus distractions into none by having it off.

2. Take the batteries out of the remote.
3. Lose the remote!
   a. Getting rid of the remote will force you to have to turn the TV on manually if you want to watch it, thus increasing the action you must take.
4. Unplug the TV.
5. Unplug the power adapter.

While this section is purposefully short and simple, endeavor each day to:

1. Identify your bad habit triggers and time sucks,
2. Think of ways to add friction to minimize or eliminate these bad habits, and
3. Find ways to make the added friction visible, enjoyable, and rewardable. ■

5. SEPARATE WORK AND PLAY SPACES

HABIT FORMATION

THE BEST WAY to break a bad habit is to remove yourself from that physical environment. There's a study on drug-addicted Vietnam veterans that showcases just how powerful a force environment is in shaping us.[30] When the soldiers left Vietnam, the likelihood of them using drugs dramatically decreased. It's the same concept for us, except our drugs are television, phone scrolling, and all other entertainment center items that exist in our homes.

This one is an extension of our earlier discussion to avoid context-mixing, but this goes beyond a physical seat or space itself and gets into the surrounding area. Let's put it this way: If you work at a table set for four and always sit at the head chair when working, and then move to the righthand chair when eating dinner or playing on your phone, you've technically, successfully, avoided context-mixing, just at a very precise level—a level so precise, it leaves a lot of room for concern and nearby failure.

Let's say you instead work in the den or office and eat dinner at the table. Now not only does it not matter which chair you use, but also it gives you clear separation. One major benefit of clear separation is that it's defined and it's visible to others. You're signaling to others when you're available based on where you are. It may sound simple, but it's powerful. If you're in the office scrolling on your phone with your feet up, both you and anyone else who's even remotely exposed to this behavior won't respect the confines of your "work" space. It's no longer an office so much as it is a place where you attempt to do work, or worse, attempt to show others you thought about doing some work.

If you avoid pretending, you'll avoid defending yourself to others about how you're "working." ∎

4. UNDERSTAND THAT NOT ALL HOURS ARE EQUAL

ONE HOUR IS not always the same. And no, I'm not making some strange reference to daylight saving time or some conspiracy theory—I understand that one hour is always sixty minutes. However, one hour spent on your homework is not the same as one hour at a networking event or one hour preparing for an interview. Heck, thirty hours on your homework isn't even remotely the same as one hour in an interview.

Despite this fact, we often treat these options as equivalent or as interchangeable in what we do and fail to do. *We confuse minutes with magnitude.*

Homework will take an hour and the networking is also listed for an hour, so that's two hours. The timeline is the same, so it gets allocated in our mind's calendar and our physical calendar(s) the same, completely blind to the impact that extra networking could have on your life, or the little impact that spending less time on a homework assignment would have.

Pursuit Decision-Making Nine-Box Matrix

	Impactability		
Probability	**6** High/Low Taking Side Job Loosely Connected to Identity Capital	**3** High/Medium Launching New Idea in a Job that Would Result in Promotion	**1** High/High Final Stages of Interview, Contract, Book Deal, etc.
	8 Medium/Low Taking Job Disconnected from Identity Capital	**4** Medium/Medium Running Event at Your Job	**2** Medium/High In Process/Warm Lead to Purpose or Economic Driver
	9 Low/Low Avoid at All Costs: Video Game Levels	**7** Low/Medium Pitching Article to Newspaper, Instagram Semi-Influencer	**5** Low/High Cold/Cool Outreach to Investor, Online Job App at Dream Co.

In order to exact our allocation, we must first understand the implication of said time. In Practice 69 we discussed the revised Eisenhower matrix with the impactability–probability (I–P) nine-box layout to determine how to spend our time, but let's take it a step further. That I–P chart can not only make us more mindful of the potential needs-payoff of our time, but it can also help us balance our time better, and it can tell us how much time to allocate to each box. For that very reason, I've updated the graphic here to include an allocation index—where to overindex your time and conversely where to underindex.

Pursuit Decision-Making Nine-Box Matrix

Probability (vertical axis)

6 High/Low Taking Side Job Loosely Connected to Identity Capital	3 High/Medium Launching New Idea In a Job that Would Result in Promotion	1 High/High Final Stages of Interview, Contract, Book Deal, etc.
8 Medium/Low Taking Job Disconnected from Identity Capital	4 Medium/Medium Running Event at Your Job	2 Medium/High In Process/Warm Lead to Purpose or Economic Driver
9 Low/Low Avoid at All Costs: Video Game Levels	7 Low/Medium Pitching Article to Newspaper, Instagram Semi-Influencer	5 Low/High Cold/Cool Outreach to Investor, Online Job App at Dream Co.

Impactability

In our Commence interviewing course, I've brought up how I've been fortunate enough to be offered the job, or the next step in the process for those I've turned down, in fifteen of my eighteen interview processes. While we have an entire course dedicated to excellence in interview preparation, if I had to summarize the number one reason why I've been able to do well in these processes, I would say it's because I overindex interview preparation. In a world where the vast majority of folks do the typical one to two hours of prep, I've done a lot more: advanced research that I happened to take two to three levels deeper past the initial anticipated question, typed up our discussion notes, mailed copies of my first book where applicable, etc.

Now you may be rolling your eyes saying that's a little aggressive. Sure, it is. Relative to societal standards, it's very aggressive. You know where it's not aggressive? It's not "doing the most" when you put it into a cost-benefit analysis.

Let's set up the scenario in simple terms. An interview process is usually the primary determinant, sometimes sole determinant, in getting a job. And it's usually based on three to eight interactions. So in simple terms, if you impress someone five out of five times, you're fairly likely to get the job. If putting in an extra two hours each time equates to ten extra hours of work, your effort is ten hours in exchange for infinite upside potential. At a minimum for most, the new job they're interviewing for represents thousands of extra dollars, so even at an extra $2,000 in first-year earnings, it's $200 per hour. Again, that's a minimum, since that uptick will compound over time, resulting in more enjoyment, benefits, and money throughout. These five instances can open the door to five years, or maybe even five decades, of opportunities for fulfillment, financial freedom, fun, and all the other F's that were failed in Practice 33's F test.

Does that extra couple hours sound crazy now?

The takeaway here is this: Don't look to society to tell you what to do. Look at what the impact would be if done well and the time difference between OK, good, and great. Look at the by-product of your efforts. The lasting effects. The magnitude of impact. ■

3. WE ONLY GET FOUR TO FIVE HOURS OF PEAK BRAIN ENERGY PER DAY—USE IT WISELY

HABIT FORMATION

LET ME KNOW if this sounds familiar. You wake up TIRED. Snooze/scroll on your phone in bed. Get ready for work, get your morning caffeine intake, make it through the work morning OK, have a relatively quick lunch indoors, and battle your circadian-rhythm afternoon slump, until you limp your way to the end of the day. Then you leave work to either walk outside, talk to friends, go to the gym, or whatever else you enjoy, just to realize: *You know what? I feel pretty good. I feel energized. Alert. Focused—I love this!* Then you get home and either watch TV, cook dinner, do chores, run errands, or some other humdrum doldrum, brain-bummed activity. You spent all day laboring, and once you hit your peak you…squandered it.

Maybe you realized it, but more than likely, you didn't. Heck, I sometimes still don't. That's just life. It follows a particular societal track that tells us evenings are for chores and relaxation—not productivity. Well, whether it's the morning, afternoon, evening, or nighttime, you need to find ways to maximize your day. Let your brain tell you when to work, not the other way around.

Feeling particularly great? Eat that biggest frog. That top task. That PQO. That dream. That legacy-leaving living.

Feeling just OK? Get the moderate tasks done.

Feeling like you're barely getting by? This is when you do the humdrum, doldrum, brain-bum, I'm feeling dumb, I'm about to succumb, how about some rum?, small sums.

This isn't just an idea or theory—it's been studied.

Dr. Isaiah Hankel, author of *The Science of Intelligent Achievement*, says there're only five hours in a day when our brain is operating at 80 percent.[31] Perhaps even more startling than that, we have only 1.5 to 2 hours each day of peak brain energy and concentration. That means that 2 out of 16 waking hours, or 12.5 percent of the time, we are at our optimal levels, and just less than half of the time (7 out of 16 hours) are we at or near optimal.

Not only is this concerning from a time perspective, but it's even more concerning from a *timing* perspective. Two hours max? What if I'm driving to work? Doing chores? Out with friends? Cooking dinner? At my daughter's dance recital? There are any number of activities that can take us away from taking advantage of our peak, so what can be done?

You can use habit stacking to make sure you're spending your time and using your energy following your PECE (Positive Energy Cultivation Exercise) on something worthwhile—not cleaning, TV, chores, etc. Allocate the time so it's not just carving out time for your PECE but also for the follow on. This works perfectly for those who can squeeze in the gym during lunch—one hour at the gym, and then 1.5 hours of peak energy at work afterward.

Another time frame to be mindful of comes from the author himself. Hankel mentions that many people reach their peaks roughly one to two hours after they wake up. If this is you, what are you doing roughly ninety minutes after waking up? Are you in your primed, non-context-mixed environment working toward your PQO? If not, audit what's holding you back. Maybe it's changing your morning work routine or your environment, or maybe your morning scrolling is setting you back so much that you're wasting your peak sitting on the subway, in traffic, or on the train into work.

Be diligent about the structure of your day so you can optimize your output. ■

GOING THE EXTRA MILE

You should address this process in four steps:

Step 1: Mindfulness. Track when you're at your mental peak. Apps like Rise can help with this.

Step 2: Hit rate. Track how often you're working on your PQO or job (if different) during this peak time.

Step 3: Utilization. Track what percentage of your peak is going toward your PQO or job, as well as how much is going toward your baseline activities (showering, eating, cleaning up, TV, etc.). Are you maximizing, stabilizing, or agonizing?

Step 4: Lag. Track how long it takes you to get into an environment to work on your PQO or job. If you get there after a nature walk, but it takes you an hour to get back to your car and another hour to get to your working environment, your mindfulness and hit rate might be high, but utilization will struggle and only come to light by tracking, and mitigating, the lag.

2. FIND, AND CONSISTENTLY CALL UPON, YOUR POSITIVE ENERGY SOURCE

ENERGY CULTIVATION

PERHAPS ONE OF the most frustrating observations I know of is this: People complain (constantly) about how tired they are and then just…linger in it, knowing full well that there are so many energy sources to tap into! They are afraid to help improve their state of being, since it's uncomfortable, unusual, or just potentially seen as uncool by those around them. One or all these factors freeze folks into a state of perpetual tiredness and further perpetuate their problems. For me, I'm often afraid of societal judgment when filming content—it makes me quite uncomfortable. I must remind myself that I only stand to gain. Not only do I stand to gain the content itself, but I could gain the passersby.

Those who think I'm crazy may give a look or mumble something on their way by, but that's just it. It's done in passing. On their way as they go on with their day. Conversely those who are intrigued? Well, they ask questions and offer their encouragement, agreement, or support! Whether it be new insights, support, friends, peers, or future investors/colleagues, we only stand to gain.

So now the question is this: What is it that gives you energy? What is it that can take you from falling asleep to producing a heap? Corny to say, but hopefully memorable. Hopefully it gets you to use those energy sources instead of defaulting to caffeine.

In the Commence program I co-founded, we use the five-minute pomodoro breaks to try various positive energy cultivation exercises. Listed are fifteen of the student favorites:

1. **Pump-up song**: Pretty self-explanatory, but what song(s) gets you energized? Ready to work? Ready to take on the world? Refer back to Practice 50 for more.

2. **Amazing human performance clips**: Sometimes to combat against complacency, it's best to watch those who are capable of absolute perfection and excellence at the highest level. This can reinspire or jolt you back into focus.

3. **Comedy skits**: A shout-out to my friend Vanessa Van Edwards here for sharing her way of dispelling nervousness: watching a comedy skit or stand-up routine. This also works for a quick pick-me-up as it gets us smiling, naturally.

4. **Getting outdoors**: Whether it's the fresh air, vitamin D, or something else—there's a whole laundry list of why this works.

5. **Power poses**: Largely known from Amy Cuddy's study, power poses increase confidence.[32] Refer back to Practice 98 for more.

6. **Combating imposter syndrome**: A helpful exercise is to call upon our most impressive successes and to reframe our less-than-successful moments by rerouting our mind from thinking they were failures to understanding they were course corrections back onto our path or opportunities to learn and improve.

7. **Designing your turbo-charged home**: This is one of the many fun exercises from Victoria Song's *Bending Reality*. You ask: "If my home only ran on things that energize and focus me, what would I put in there? What would I take out?"[33]

8. **Meditation**: Meditation, which I've come to learn is largely concentrating solely on your breath and body, can be done anywhere, any time. Much like prayer, it's something we like to think is harder than it really is. The more you do it, the better you'll get, but don't let newness scare you away from trying. It just might help.

9. **4-7-8 breathing**: This is my favorite breathing technique. Its cadence follows: Inhale for 4 seconds, hold the breath for 7 seconds, and slowly exhale for 8 seconds. While it sounds simple, exhaling for 8 seconds can be a challenge, so this exercise really forces relaxation (bit of an oxymoron there) and intentionality, since you're forced to count the 8 seconds.

10. **Positive visualization exercise**: Oprah, Arnold, Jim Carrey—many swear by the power of positive visualization. To harness the full power of positive visualizations, think of your visualization process

as detailing a suspect to the police: The more you share and the more you call upon visualization to produce this image, the clearer it gets. The clearer it gets, the more likely the suspect will be apprehended. Think of your dream as a fleeting suspect whose image gets a little fuzzier each week you don't craft the mental picture. Envision the life, career, or just result you want, and your continuous, recurring focus on that goal makes it more likely to happen.

Positive visualization doesn't have to stop at dreams—it can extend into your daily practices as well. The peak performance expert Anders Ericsson explained this well in his studies of mental representations and how to make actions and associations as efficient and clear as possible. He wrote, "Much of deliberate practice involves developing ever more efficient mental representations that you can use in whatever activity you are practicing."[34] In this way you can think of mental representations as the granular, vivid version of visualization. The clearer the picture, more descriptive the mental process, and less time it takes to call upon this vision, the better it is and the more likely you are to succeed.

11. **Sound (bath) therapy**: ASMR has taken off, and it's no surprise—we as humans are sensitive to sounds, perhaps a lot more than we realize. Taking a sound bath—I recommend the crystal bowls one—is a spa-like experience for your ears and peace of mind.

12. **Note to your future self**: My favorite high school exercise (thank you, Mr. Necio) was writing a note to my future, five-years-from-now self. Its benefits are fourfold. It:
    a. Gets you to prioritize what you want in life.
    b. Puts a timetable on improvement, something we often don't have time stamps for postgraduation.
    c. Puts pen to paper: Writing something down increases commitment.
    d. Creates curiosity and commitment via future predictions. We all like it when we have our moments of clairvoyance, so this note to our future selves is a unique commitment device for us to follow through and explore our passions.

13. **Beautiful imagery**: Whether it's something tranquil to relax us, something one-of-a-kind to inspire us, or something extravagant that helps to motivate us, beautiful imagery can be a powerful tool if used in proportionality—enough to reap the benefits above, but not too much that it makes us materialistic or sad about our perceived lack.

14. **Self-affirmations**: I put together a list of fifty powerful self-affirmations and ask students to find five that appeal to them because, as Dr. Julie Smith points out, using an affirmation you don't believe in has a negative (not neutral) impact on us, making it critical to find three to five that we can feel personally empowered by.[35]

15. **List of microjoys**: What are the renewable, frequent things in life that bring you joy? A happy puppy? Purring cat? Clapping baby? Summer sunset? Write down ten to twenty items you can use to brighten your day (on command). ■

I. KEEP THIS LIST, AND OTHER PRODUCTIVITY BOOKS, VISIBLE AND OBVIOUS

HABIT FORMATION

KEITH FERRAZZI SAID "…You'll get the most from this book if your desire to learn is exceeded only by your willingness to act."[36]

In other words, be steadfast in your pursuit of improvement. For fellow Marvel fans, think of this list as your own personal army of Avengers—avenging all the time stolen from you one way or another. Like the Hulk, Iron Man, or Scarlet Witch, each one of these principles has its own strength, use case, and of course, personal appeal. Employ what works for you and use the army of options to your advantage, as the Thanos of Thought Prevention or the Ultron of Unproductive is not only strong but inevitable.

If you need help figuring out which skills to prioritize, ask yourself this question from Dr. Julie Smith: "Imagine that far into the future you were near the end of your life and looking back on this chapter that is just beginning. If you were to look back with a smile on your face, feeling content and satisfied with the choices you made and the way you approached each day, what would daily life need to look like? The answer to that question enlists your priorities."[37]

With one hundred practices available, it's important to know that no one is expecting you to do them all, as, quite frankly, you cannot. The audits and analysis alone would prevent you from maximizing your output. My advice to you would be to flip back through the book and see where you highlighted, commented, starred, exclamation pointed, circled, and asterisked most, and then apply the famed 80/20 principle. In Richard Koch's book *The 80/20 Principle* he points out how 80 percent of revenues are driven by 20 percent of clients and 80 percent of our work product is done in 20 percent of our time. In other words, how do we focus our time, attention, and efforts on what's going to be our biggest yield?

One hundred ideas? Too much to implement. Choosing twenty ideas to focus on? Much more palatable.

My suggestion would be to find your top twenty ideas and then rank them. After they're ranked, build a starter plan of ten ideas and order them by which you will attempt first. Focusing on only ten of the twenty practices means you have a backup or reserve bank of ten additional ideas that can step in to replace the ideas that don't work well for you. This book points out ways to combat many problems, but it should be personal to your needs. Think of your issues: Is your problem getting started, sustaining effort, or finishing (strong)? Build a chronology to help with all three stages, but stack your primary focus on the area you struggle with most. For instance, if it's sustaining that's your issue, put together a plan that's two ideas for getting started, five for sustaining, and three for finishing. Try to ensure that your backup ten ideas have options for these three buckets as well so you can easily plug and play as you work to figure out how to create your *maximized* life.

With all content complete, let me be the first to say I'm proud of you. To purchase, read, and complete a self-development book puts you in the minority of not only people, but even of readers. It puts you in rarefied air. But this is only the beginning. Before reaching for any one of the great books I referenced here, I encourage you to make an action plan and take action. To inspire action, instill confidence, and impugn any potential imposter syndrome, let's close with a quick yet powerful reminder of the power you hold, the infinite potential you carry, and the impact you can have:

"You are here to enable the divine purpose of the universe to unfold, that's how important you are."
—ECKHART TOLLE[38] ▪

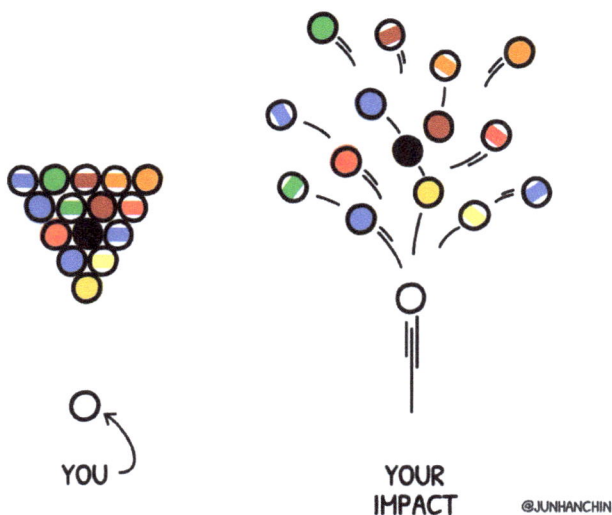

YOU

YOUR
IMPACT   @JUNHANCHIN

Congratulations on making it to this point! You not only sought out this book—you read it thoroughly and you *finished* it. You should feel proud of your commitment to bettering yourself. To keep your progress moving forward, and to ensure your continuous commitment, tell five people about how you finished this book and the top five steps you're going to take.

Capitalize on this right now. I've given you this extra page to serve as your own habit contract. Sign your name and date it to mark this ceremonious occasion. Below it, write down your top five skills to focus on, alongside five to twenty more you'd like to consider. Do it right now—it might just make you $500.

Your name: _____

Signature: _____

Date: _____

Five people to tell: _____

_____

Top five priorities:

	Getting Started	Sustaining Effort	Finishing Strong	Optimizing Output
1				
2				
3				
4				
5				

Future priorities/other strong considerations:

	Getting Started	Sustaining Effort	Finishing Strong	Optimizing Output
1				
2				
3				
4				
5				
6				
7				
8				
9				
10				

Social Media Post Options

X: Just finished reading *Maximize* by Alex Dripchak and taking immediate action to implement better routines in life by challenging myself to do (*insert your top goal or practice here*) by (*sample date*). Who can help keep me accountable that day or along the way?

I've got this goal to do X by *month, day, year*, and I need an accountability partner. Will anyone be my social media date? I'll split the winnings with you. 😊

Instagram: I just finished reading *Maximize: A Playbook-Style Countdown of the Top 100 Productivity Practices,* and my five action items are:

1.
2.
3.
4.
5.

Who can help keep me accountable so I can do more and do it better, more consistently, and at peak energy levels? Better yet, who else will join me in trying to transform?

Imagine a world where people are performing 50 percent better. Even easier, imagine what could happen if we did just 5 percent better. Maybe on the path to maximize we land on optimize or right-size. Whether incremental or monumental, imagine what we can do as a society with every reader doing just a little more, doing it just a little better and just a little clearer. What could we improve? What could we fix? What could we solve? What could we course-correct? That's why I'm rooting for you! For a chance to win, enter our drawings with a picture of your copy of Maximize *and one of the sample posts above or a custom post. Refer to the following platforms for more information:*

- TikTok: adultingmadeasy
- Instagram: areyouworkforceready
- LinkedIn: The Commence Foundation

THE NEXT BEST 11 AND FULL LIST OF POSITIVE ENERGY CULTIVATORS

JUST MISSED THE CUT

Don't Let Most Apps Send You Banner Notifications

TIME MANAGEMENT

Chances are you aren't a political news correspondent and therefore you don't have to see the latest political scandal news alert. Chances are also pretty high that you're not a sports agent who needs to see the latest terms of a top athlete's contract immediately.

It can wait.

Yet for 81 percent of users, it doesn't.

According to a 2021 study by Airship, opt-in rates for banner notifications, or your phone's version of a breaking news alert, were a median of 81 percent of Android users (where it's the default) and 51 percent for the opt-in iOS users who proactively select it.[39] An even more astounding study showed 33 percent of eighteen- to thirty-four-year-olds *always* allow push notifications.[40] No wonder why younger generations are on their phones so much—it's hard to put them down when they're constantly buzzing with new alerts!

As Herbert Simon says, "A wealth of information creates a poverty of attention."[41] The more overloaded with information you are, and the more stimuli you're engulfed in, the more distracted and inattentive you become.

So what should you do? Stop the buzzing and stop the banner, home screen alerts. Ask yourself, *What alerts do I absolutely need to have as soon as they break?* Or better yet, ask yourself what you would miss if you didn't get an alert immediately. The list is surprisingly short.

For those asking why—*Why should I go out of my way* (especially for Android users) *to turn these off? I'm so used to them anyway that I barely even notice them.* Well, for one, they're still a distraction. You're still most likely reading the alerts and thinking about them or lingering on them for a minute.

Second, it breaks your rhythm, or worse, your prized flow. Now this isn't true of all phone notifications but here I'm going to single out the home/lock screen because if you see something you're interested in, say the terms of Justin Jefferson's new contract, you click the link. You read the report. And before you know it, you're searching for other wide receivers' contract terms. Then the highest-paid players in the NFL. Then dissecting which of those are on your favorite team. Texting your fellow team followers and fans about the news, and your findings, and maybe some what-ifs or can-you-imagines. Long story short, it gets you down a rabbit hole and it keeps you there searching for Little Peter Cottontail. It also gets you picking up your phone constantly, and what happens when you pick up your phone? Well, you text…you scroll…you social…you… sometimes just carousel around screens and ask ten minutes later—why am I on my phone?

As you know from earlier, it's easy to do, because, after all, your phone is more of an entertainment center than an education or productivity platform, and if you don't have the guardrails on tight, the easier and more immediately enjoyable option will win out.

If It's Going to Take Less than Five Minutes—Do It Now

TIME MANAGEMENT

One of the easiest ways to cheat your own productivity is to make a to-do list of many one-to-four-minute, one-off activities.

Let's review why.

Well, for starters, you took a minute to write it down. Took another minute to revisit it at a later point in time, which inevitably leads to a minute to think about it.

Say you then accomplish it—you get a dopamine hit from accomplishing one of the ten things you had on your to-do list. One of ten. *Regardless of what else is on that list, 10 percent of it is already done* is what your brain has just told you. By putting it as a to-do task, it'll make you feel, artificially, more productive, and this simple act of calendaring may have increased the task's to-do time-frame by upward of 300 percent.

Calendaring would take too long.

The mental load and distraction would cost you too much.

In short, if it needs to get done and it would take less than five minutes to do it, take care of it at your very first opportunity.

Consider the amount of lost time spent thinking about the task you need to do, the lack of focus taking you away from your best work, or the inability to fall asleep because it's weighing on you. Whatever that small, one-off task is, avoid it by accomplishing it. Like right now. I'll wait.

Find Ways to Minimize Decision Fatigue

MOTIVATION AND ALIGNMENT

There's a famous story about Mark Zuckerberg and how he has a wardrobe of many versions of his favorite go-to outfits. His reason? It's one less thing to have to decide on. Well, his exact words are, "I feel like I'm not doing my job if I spend any of my energy on things that are silly or frivolous about my life."[42]

Jay Shetty talks more about this in his book *Think like a Monk* when discussing how having specific actions or calls to action on set days and times allows you to focus on other tasks and opens you up to being more creative.[43]

While Shetty, Zuckerberg, and many others have mastered the minimization of decision fatigue, it's author Barry Schwartz who is our paramount expert. Schwartz writes in his book *The Paradox of Choice* that having more choices has confounded us in many ways. More choices, to many, means more "wrong" answers, and those wrong choices often translate to the amplification of perceived consequences. All this has led to less enjoyment, which in turn produces less overall happiness for us.

In whatever area you may struggle with making decisions, limit your options.

Work on Your Posture

MOTIVATION AND ALIGNMENT

Akin to how nice attire can help give you a mental boost,[44] good posture can also help prime you for success. The simplest way good posture can be achieved is by standing. Not only does standing have health benefits, but it's also been shown to potentially increase engagement and focus.

If standing isn't for you, consider that proper posture also helps you avoid muscle strain or fatigue. Whether you're less productive due to injuries sidelining you from being your best self, or the hours lost to rehabilitate your injury in physical therapy, bad posture has ripple effects.

Have Your Caffeine Ninety Minutes After Waking Up

TIME MANAGEMENT

When waking up in the morning, your adenosine levels are low since you're well rested.[45] Therefore experts recommend waiting ninety minutes before consuming your morning cup.[46] This enables you to take advantage of the alertness you have coming out of bed, allows your adenosine to rise to levels that allow caffeine to be more effective, and prevents caffeine from disrupting your natural cortisol rhythm. All this to say, there are many reasons why you're better off waiting before getting your caffeine fix. Just don't wait too long—caffeine is recommended to be curtailed six to eight hours before bed.[47]

When Needed, Do a Caffeine Boost of Drink + Sleep

TIME MANAGEMENT

In the moments you find yourself completely exhausted, needing to spring into action soon, and exercise is not possible, plan to do a caffeine boost. This means getting yourself set up for a nap with comfortable attire, a dark space, and a relaxed mindset. As soon as you're all prepped, drink your caffeine quickly, and immediately upon finishing your cup, nap for twenty to twenty-five minutes.[48] The combination will allow you to "double up" the surge you'd see from a nap as well as from a cup of coffee or tea.

It's important to prep your environment first though, as caffeine takes at least five (but more research supports fifteen) minutes to take effect. It may sound like a lot, but falling asleep often takes just as long.

Go See a Body of Water

ENERGY CULTIVATION

Blue calms us. Water creates a sense of awe. A body of water also provides a place for relaxation with its sounds and waves. There are many studies and hypotheses about the wide-reaching effects of proximity to water and blue spaces, and while the results are mixed, psychosocial well-being has been shown to improve with exposure to bodies of water.

So to relax and refocus, go enjoy time near a body of water. You might also notice benefits of mindfulness, reflection, and even enhanced physical activity.

Align Tasks by Time of Day

TIME MANAGEMENT

Experts say we are more ready to analyze in the mornings and more apt to create or think creatively in the evenings. While everyone has their own chronotype, how can you apply these guidelines to your day? Well, we covered some in the book, but to best understand what's good for you, you might want to consider taking a page out of author Chris Bailey's *The Productivity Project*.

Chris advises readers to cut caffeine and alcohol, minimize sugar, and even skip the alarm clock for a couple weeks and track each waking hour's energy level. Without the stimulants, or depressants, and without the alarm, you will get to know your body as it intends. The practicality of cutting so much in one fell swoop might not be feasible for many readers, so this one falls outside our top 100 practices. But, for the real go-getters looking for a challenge and a journey toward personal energy enlightenment, this is a good one to try.

Avoid Sitting Longer than Thirty Minutes at a Time

TIME MANAGEMENT

...And less than eight hours a day. Not only does it tire you and lull you into the unproductive, but in a 2018 study published by PLOS One, it's been correlated to a thinner medial temporal lobe (MTL).[49] The MTL is an area of the brain tied to memory, and thin MTLs are believed to potentially play a role as a precursor to cognitive decline. Since this practice is more about keeping your years as maximized as possible, as opposed to tips for each day, week, or month—coupled with how it's not always practical to walk around every thirty minutes—this one just missed the cut.

Put Your Phone on Airplane Mode

TIME MANAGEMENT

One of the simplest yet most powerful tips. If you can't fully commit to airplane mode in case you might be needed at a second's notice, try Do Not Disturb or set up a Focus setting on your phone that you can set by time or location.

Nir Eyal in *Indistractable* tells us to try and abide by the ten-minute rule: If you feel the urge to check your phone, wait ten minutes and then see if the urge is still there.[50] You're not only unknowingly implementing the 10/1 productivity method but also learning to break the knee-jerk reaction to check your phone relentlessly. With stimuli constantly increasing, and attention spans consistently decreasing, impulse control might just become the next big professional skill in demand.

Set Restrictions from Your Phone, Not Inside the App

TIME MANAGEMENT

A simple yet powerful practice. App-based restrictions are pretty easy to ignore. Why? Well, because they want you to engage with them more. Set restrictions from your phone settings, as it's also a more powerful measure. Sometimes even if we do stick to the limits within an app, say Instagram, we just migrate over to Twitter, Facebook, TikTok, Snapchat, Pinterest, etc., to keep our scrolling/content consumption habit(s) alive. Then who knows—maybe you find you actually miss those apps or discover something you really enjoy about one of their new features, and instead of curtailing a social media addiction, you're actually fueling it, and the battle has gotten even more difficult. Set the restrictions on social channels (add in things like WhatsApp too) and you'll be especially diligent. After all, so much time, so few apps. Strike that. Reverse it.

If you're looking for a level-up beyond this time restriction, there's an app called ClearSpace that's worth a shot. The concept of having to take a specified number of steps or do push-ups to unlock apps like Instagram or Netflix is a terrific time restriction mechanism but an even better temptation bundling example, not dissimilar to that which Ronan Byrne introduced us to in Practice 30.

POSITIVE ENERGY CULTIVATORS

For those of you who liked our 15 energy cultivators from Practice number 2 here's our full list of 64 positive energy cultivators.

1. Exercising
2. Walking
3. Jogging
4. Calisthenics/jumping jacks
5. Running
6. Weight lifting
7. Interval training
8. Exercise classes
9. Cycling/stationary biking
10. Swimming
11. Playing a sport
12. Getting outside
13. Going into nature
14. Sunbathing
15. Looking up at the sky
16. Looking at a body of water
17. Microjoy (sunset, dog, baby, kitten, etc.)
18. Joy on demand
19. Beautiful imagery
20. Inspiring places to see
21. Impressive performances
22. Personal highlight reel
23. Key word/phrase to remind yourself of a great moment or time in your life
24. Comedy skit
25. Talking to a friend
26. Talking to a family member
27. Talking to the elderly
28. Deep breathing
29. Meditating
30. Sauna or steam room

31. Yoga
32. Stretching
33. Power posing
34. Binaural beats
35. Sound bath
36. ASMR
37. Cathartic screaming
38. Coping audit
39. Vagus nerve reset/clavicle stroking
40. Relaxing music
41. Classical music
42. Pump-up music
43. Inspirational music
44. Favorite music
45. Positive visualizing
46. Five senses—dream-come-true feeling
47. Miracle/miracle healing exercise—what would you do differently?
48. Turbocharged home—positives and negatives to power your home
49. Self-affirmations
50. Combating imposter syndrome
51. Three good things activity
52. Gratitude journaling
53. Addressing setbacks
54. Writing
55. Journaling
56. Personal mission statement
57. Note to future self
58. List making
59. Goal setting
60. Meaning, purpose, skills exercise
61. Tea
62. Coffee
63. Snack
64. Water

In *Hidden Potential*, Adam Grant quotes Eric Best: Did you make yourself better today? Did you make someone else better today? If the answer to either question is yes, it was a good day.[51]

ACKNOWLEDGMENTS

What started off as a curiosity about how many words my speaking notes to our course on productivity was has become a finished book, and I have a great number of people to thank for it.

Perhaps most surprisingly, the first person I have to thank is someone I've never met: Jim Kwik. Jim's book *Limitless* caught me and a great many others during an unprecedented time—the first weeks of the COVID-19 pandemic in the New York Metro area. We were a captive audience, in more ways than one. While I've always been focused on being present, productive, and passionate, Jim's work kicked it into overdrive and served as the launching point for my self-development book reading and personal journey. Doubling my reading speed and introducing me to the memory palace and a host of excellent practices and practitioners, Jim's work has left a lasting impression. This book and my foundation would likely not exist without his work. Thank you, Jim.

I think I speak for anyone who writes on productivity or any related topic that we must acknowledge the patriarchs of productivity and performance: Anders Ericsson (and Robert Pool) and Mihaly Csikszentmihalyi. *Peak* and *Flow* remain as two of the most foundational books, and cited sources, for us all. Thank you for opening up the gateway to greater understanding, application, research, and practice.

Along the lines of Mihaly and Anders, I must thank those like Jim who have made productivity cool. Yes, I'm looking at you, James Clear, Brendon Burchard, Mel Robbins, Stephen Covey, David Allen, and many others. Beyond productivity, ever-present authors like Ryan Holiday, James Altucher, Dale Carnegie, Eckhart Tolle, and Jay Shetty have a knack for making their way into all self-development book citations. With powerful influencers like these, writing this book was as streamlined as possible; thank you for sharing your wise words and powerful practices with the world. I hope you enjoy the evolutions here as well as the new ideas!

I'd be remiss if I didn't thank my friends, colleagues, and connections who not only provide their support but their time, expertise, and encouragement for the Commence Foundation. It's because of wonderful people like you that I'm hopeful we can do our part to help fix the lack of curricula, knowledge, and understanding of life's most powerful skills: the essential life skills. With so many (more) impressive professionals and writers, it's easy to let the foreboding shadow and dark cloud of imposter syndrome keep me from publishing this book, but it is your reminders, genuine remarks, and appreciation for the Commence vision that have propelled me forward. While the builder-uppers and risers know who they are, a special shoutout to Chris McGlade, John and Gabrielle D'Arco, Xavier Roliz, Chris and Aileen King, Nick Gregoretti, Keith and Lauren Dore, Connie Von Zwehl, and Cody Reid.

Productivity starts at a young age, and as every study shows us of great performers, they have an exceptional model to follow from a young age. While I'm not sure I've achieved great performer status just yet, I did have the benefit of an exceptional model at home: my father (and financial wellness colead), David Dripchak. It's crazy to think in our hybrid, work-from-home world of today that for years my dad drove (one way) either 106 miles or 163 miles to work, putting him on the road before 5:00 a.m. each day. Productivity and performance require two other P's—persistence and perseverance—and I had these as a front-and-center frame of reference to lead my life. Parents out there: The example you set provides a frame of reference, if not a benchmark, if not a "record to beat" in your kids' heads, so make a firm commitment to excellence. It will likely help you but even more impactfully, it just might motivate your kids for eighty years to come like it has, and will continue to, for me.

Of course, it takes both a model and a support system to make it happen, and when it comes to a support system, they don't make 'em any better than my mom, Susan Dripchak. Just about every time I call, I'm not only greeted with an excited remark but it's almost always immediately followed with a comment to my dad of, "Turn that down! It's Alex." When you have someone relentlessly interested in your endeavors, it not only helps stoke the coals as you burn the midnight oil, but it subtly forces you to work more consistently and frequently. So, in a less obvious way, I have my mom's eager interest to thank for my productivity.

It's rare to find anyone who is going to care about your endeavors, interests, and pursuits as much as your mother, but that's one of the many things I get to appreciate about my wonderful wife, Nesha. After some of the more severe, and scary, health episodes I've had, Nesha has not only been there for research, comfort, love, and support but also to reiterate how she'd carry the Commence Foundation torch for me if I was unable to do so myself. This is, and likely always will be, the greatest gesture I've seen in my life, and for that I extend my most profound thank-you.

I'll end my acknowledgments with perhaps the most welcomed, and scheduled, distraction of all: my son Colton! The irony of publishing a book on productivity while having an infant is not lost on me, and while newborns can be quite a strain on what you may accomplish in the short term, they are an infinitely powerful source of purpose.

Colton, you have a smile that eviscerates tension, a laugh that apexes joy, a scent that emits a superpower of strength, and a sound that unlocks incomparable love. I thank you for being my motivation source.

I can't wait to acknowledge you, my readers, through our interactions in person and on social. I know there's a vast treasure trove of inspired, purposeful people out there seeking to do more for others, and the collective greater good, and I can hardly wait to meet you. I leave this white space for all those I've yet to meet.

Onward and upward,

"And whatever you do, whether in word or deed, do it all in the name of the Lord Jesus, giving thanks to God the Father through him."
—COLOSSIANS 3:17

NOTES

Part I. 100–76: Improving Your Day to Day

1   Robert Cialdini, *Influence: The Psychology of Persuasion* (William Morrow, 1998), 3.

2   Michael J. Breus, "Chronoquiz: What's Your Chronotype?" Sleep Doctor, updated October 7, 2024, https://sleepdoctor.com/pages/chronotypes/chronotype-quiz.

3   Astrid Schütz and Brad Bushman, "88 Studies of Power Poses Reveal Whether They Work or Not," Fast Company, June 12, 2022, https://www.fastcompany.com/90760166/88-studies-of-power-poses-reveal-whether-they-work-or-not.

4   Madeline Miles, "Power Poses: How to Feel More Confident with Body Language," *Better Up* (blog), May 2, 2023, https://www.betterup.com/blog/power-poses.

5   Ric Elias, interview by Peter Attia, *The Drive*, episode 79, "Ric Elias: Earning the Gift of Life," November 11, 2019, https://peterattiamd.com/ricelias/.

6   Colin P. West et al., "Association of Resident Fatigue and Distress with Perceived Medical Errors," *Journal of American Medicine* 302, no. 12 (September 2009): 1294–1300, https://doi.org/10.1001/jama.2009.1389.

7   Meghan Overdeep, "Stop Complaining, It's Literally Shrinking Your Brain," Yahoo!Life, July 17, 2019, https://www.yahoo.com/lifestyle/stop-complaining-literally-shrinking-brain-181731777.html.

8   Jay Shetty, *Think like a Monk* (Mindquest Press, 2024), 33.

9   Mark Manson, *The Subtle Art of Not Giving a F*ck: A Counterintuitive Approach to Living a Good Life* (Harper One, 2016), 9–11.

10 Brendon Burchard, *High Performance Habits: How Extraordinary People Became That Way* (Hay House, 2017), 188–193.

11 Norman Vincent Peale, *The Power of Positive Thinking* (Prentice-Hall, 1952), 116.

12 Malcolm Gladwell, *Outliers: The Story of Success* (Little, Brown and Company, 2008); Anders Ericsson and Robert Pool, *Peak: Secrets from the New Science of Expertise* (Mariner Books, 2017).

13   Jeff Haden, "Science Says Stop Infecting Other People with the Better-Than-Average Effect," *Inc.*, October 12, 2020, https://www.inc.com/jeff-haden/science-says-stop-infecting-other-people-with-better-than-average-effect.html.

14   Patrick Bet-David, *Your Next Five Moves: Master the Art of Business Strategy* (Gallery Books, 2020), 18–20.

15   Ryan Holiday, *The Obstacle Is the Way: The Timeless Art of Turning Trials into Triumph* (Penguin Random House, 2014), 92.

16   Burchard, *High Performance Habits*, 156.

Part II. 75–51: Becoming Your Best Self

1   Marshall Goldsmith and Mark Reiter, *Triggers: Creating Behavior That Lasts—Becoming the Person You Want to Be* (Crown, 2015), xv.

2   James Clear, *Atomic Habits: An Easy and Proven Way to Build Good Habits and Break Bad Ones* (Avery, 2018) 201.

3   Gloria Mark et al., "No Task Left Behind? Examining the Nature of Fragmented Work," paper presented at CHI 2005, Portland, OR, April 2–7, 2005, https://ics.uci.edu/~gmark/CHI2005.pdf.

4   "What Is Flow State and How Do You Achieve It?," Cigna Healthcare blog, October 4, 2022, https://www.cignaglobal.com/blog/body-mind/getting-into-a-flow-state-of-mind.

5   Inspired by Burchard, *High Performance Habits*.

6   Quote by Stephen Covey: "The main thing is to keep the main thing the ma…"

7   Phillippa Lally et al., "How Are Habits Formed: Modelling Habit Formation in the Real World," *European Journal of Social Psychology* 40, no. 6 (July 2009): 998–1009, https://doi.org/10.1002/ejsp.674.

8   Clear, *Atomic Habits*, 201.

9   Lan Phan, *Do This Daily: Secrets to Finding Success, Happiness, and Purpose in Work and Life* (Thin Leaf, 2023), 169.

10   Victoria Song, *Bending Reality: How to Make the Impossible Probable* (Forefront Books, 2021), 44.

11   Eckhart Tolle, *The Power of Now: A Guide to Spiritual Enlightenment* (Namaste Publishing, 1997), 168.

12   Brené Brown, *Daring Greatly: How the Courage to Be Vulnerable Transforms the Way We Live, Love, Parent, and Lead* (Gotham Books, 2012), 177.

13   Phan, *Do This Daily*, 173.

Part III. 50–26: Optimizing Your Lifestyle

1   Jim Kwik, *Limitless: Upgrade Your Brain, Learn Anything Faster, and Unlock Your Exceptional Life* (Hay House, 2020), 203.

2   Kiersten Willis, "Trying to Quit Caffeine? Study Says Exercise Could Have Same Effect on Brain as Coffee," *Atlanta Journal-Constitution*, January 31, 2020, https://www.ajc.com/lifestyles/health/trying-quit-caffeine-study-says-exercise-

could-have-same-effect-brain-coffee/KkOqgkW7jFes6dRt33cyNM/; "Exercise Versus Caffeine: Which Is Your Best Ally to Fight Fatigue?," *Harvard Health Publishing*, June 8, 2017, https://www.health.harvard.edu/blog/exercise-versus-caffeine-which-is-your-best-ally-to-fight-fatigue-2017060811843.

3   Julia C. Basso and Wendy A. Suzuki, "The Effects of Acute Exercise on Mood, Cognition, Neurophysiology, and Neurochemical Pathways: A Review," *Brain Plasticity* 2, no. 2 (March 2017):127–152, https://doi.org/10.3233/BPL-160040.

4   Cristopher Bergland, "The Brain-Boosting Benefits of Exercise and Cerebral Blood Flow," *Psychology Today*, May 20, 2020, https://www.psychologytoday.com/us/blog/the-athletes-way/202005/the-brain-boosting-benefits-exercise-and-cerebral-blood-flow.

5   "Boost Your Blood Flow, Get Your Memory Back," Amen Clinics, January 5, 2024, https://www.amenclinics.com/blog/memory-rescue-blood-flow/.

6   "The Best Nootropic Supplements to (Maybe) Boost Brain Power," *Healthline*, accessed October 15, 2025, https://www.healthline.com/nutrition/best-nootropic-brain-supplements.

7   National Institutes of Health Office of Dietary Supplements, *Dietary Supplements for Exercise and Athletic Performance*, updated April 1, 2024, https://ods.od.nih.gov/factsheets/ExerciseAndAthleticPerformance-HealthProfessional/.

8   Romie Mushtaq, *The Busy Brain Cure: The Eight-Week Plan to Find Focus, Tame Anxiety, and Sleep Again* (Hanover Square Press, 2024), 159.

9   Garrett Schaffel, "Leafy Greens Can Save Your Memory," AARP, March 14, 2018, https://www.aarp.org/health/brain-health/info-2018/vegetables-brain-health-fd.html.

10   Héctor García and Francesc Miralles, *Ikigai: The Japanese Secret to a Long and Happy Life* (Penguin, 2016), 130.

11   Soyogu Yamashita et al., "Effects of Egg Yolk Choline Intake on Cognitive Functions and Plasma Choline Levels in Healthy Middle-Aged and Older Japanese: A Randomized Double-Blinded Placebo-Controlled Parallel-Group Study," *Lipids in Health and Disease* 22 (June 2023), 75, https://doi.org/10.1186/s12944-023-01844-w.

12   "Information about the Brain," NIH Curriculum Supplement Series [Internet] (2007), https://www.ncbi.nlm.nih.gov/books/NBK20367/.

13   Rachel Reiff Ellis, "It's Not 8 Glasses a Day Anymore. Here's How Much Water You Should Drink Each Day," *Fortune*, May 25, 2025, https://fortune.com/well/2023/05/06/how-much-much-water-you-should-drink-each-day/.

14   Nancy Oliveira, "Water," The Nutrition Source, Harvard T.H. Chan School of Public Health, last modified February 26, 2025, https://nutritionsource.hsph.harvard.edu/water/

15   Markham Heid, "Why Drinking Water All Day Long Is Not the Best Way to Stay Hydrated," *Time*, August 9, 2019, https://time.com/5646632/how-much-water-to-drink/.

16   Clear, *Atomic Habits*, 201.

17   BJ Fogg, "Welcome to Tiny Habits," Tiny Habits, accessed September 19, 2025, https://tinyhabits.com/welcome.

18 Hannah Yasharoff, "What Is the 6-Second Kiss Rule and How Can It Give Your Relationship a Boost?," *USA Today*, June 8, 2023, https://www.usatoday.com/story/life/health-wellness/2023/06/08/6-second-kiss-theory-20-second-hug-relationship-tip/70292502007/.

19 Kirsten M. M. Beyer et al., "Time Spent Outdoors, Activity Levels, and Chronic Disease among American Adults," *Journal of Behavior Medicine* 41 (January 2018): 494–503, https://doi.org/10.1007/s10865-018-9911-1.

20 Amy S. McDonnell and David L. Strayer, "The Influence of a Walk in Nature on Human Resting Brain Activity: A Randomized Controlled Trial," *Scientific Reports* 14 (2024): 27253, https://doi.org/10.1038/s41598-024-78508-x.

21 "7 Health Benefits of Spending Time in Nature," UCLA Health, May 14, 2025, https://www.uclahealth.org/news/article/7-health-benefits-spending-time-nature.

22 "Signs You're Struggling with Cognitive Dissonance," Cleveland Clinic, November 26, 2024, https://health.clevelandclinic.org/cognitive-dissonance.

23 Chad Brooks, "Two-Day Thanksgiving Holiday Remains Popular Among Employers," Business News Daily, November 13, 2023, https://www.businessnewsdaily.com/8601-working-on-thanksgiving.html.

24 Kineree Shah, "Retail Store Closures Rise but In-Person Shopping Still Holds Strong," YouGov, March 25, 2025, https://business.yougov.com/content/51877-retail-store-closures-rise-but-in-person-shopping-still-hold-strong.

25 Simon Sinek, *Start with Why: How Great Leaders Inspire Everyone to Take Action* (Portfolio, 2009), 94–95.

26 Inspiration for this section is Shetty, *Think like a Monk*, 45.

27 Stephen R. Covey, *The 7 Habits of Highly Effective People* (Simon & Schuster, 1989), 295.

28 Manson, *The Subtle Art of Not Giving a F*ck*, 9–11.

29 Andrew D. Huberman (@hubermanlab), "The only thing we can truly control is where we place our attention and where we place our effort. Choose wisely," X, August 9, 2023, 4:06 p.m., https://x.com/hubermanlab/status/1689367451300147201.

30 Ray Dalio, *Principles* (Avid Reader Press, 2017), 156.

31 Tyler W. Watts et al., "Revisiting the Marshmallow Test: A Conceptual Replication Investigating Links Between Early Delay of Gratification and Later Outcomes," *Psychological Science* 29, no. 7 (May 2018): 1159–1177, https://doi.org/10.1177/0956797618761661.

32 "New Years Resolution Project," Quirkology, accessed September 19, 2025, http://www.richardwiseman.com/quirkology/new/USA/Experiment_resolution.shtml.

33 "Televisions Inflation Calculator," Official Data Foundation, accessed September 19, 2025, https://www.in2013dollars.com/Televisions/price-inflation/2000-to-2024.

34 Pew Research Center, *Mobile Fact Sheet* (November 13, 2024), https://www.pewresearch.org/internet/fact-sheet/mobile/.

35 Mike Winters, "How Much Money Americans Have in Their Savings Accounts—Nearly Half Have Less than $500," CNBC, January 24, 2024,

https://www.cnbc.com/2024/01/24/how-much-money-americans-have-in-savings.html.

36   D. Elizabeth, "This Exercise Bike Lets You Watch Netflix, Unless You Stop Pedaling," *Self*, August 2, 2017, https://www.self.com/story/cycflix-exercise-bike.

37   Peter Cappelli and Anna Tavis, "The Performance Management Revolution," *Harvard Business Review*, October 2016, https://hbr.org/2016/10/the-performance-management-revolution.

38   Melanie Curtin, "In an 8-Hour Day, the Average Worker Is Productive for This Many Hours," *Inc.*, accessed July 21, 2016, https://www.inc.com/melanie-curtin/in-an-8-hour-day-the-average-worker-is-productive-for-this-many-hours.html.

39   Kathy Morris, "Here's How Many Hours Workers Are Actually Productive (And What They're Doing Instead)," Zippia, January 23, 2023, https://www.zippia.com/advice/average-productive-hours-per-day/.

40   Grace Key, "How Many Hours Work Day Productive Tech Workers," *Business Insider*, May 30, 2023, https://www.businessinsider.com/how-many-hours-work-day-productive-tech-workers-2023-4.

41   Curtin, "In an 8-Hour Day."

42   Sachin Isaacs, personal communication.

43   Seneca, "On the Shortness of Life," in *Dialogues and Essays*, trans. John Davie (Oxford University Press, 2007).

44   George Papzoglou, "Unleash Your Inner Power: Exploring the Depths of Your Subconscious," Articles Factory, May 3, 2024, https://www.articlesfactory.com/articles/motivational/open-the-pandoras-box-unleash-your-hidden-inside-power.html.

45   emthie23, "Moving from Autopilot Towards Mindfulness," *CogBlog—A Cognitive Psychology Blog*, November 24, 2020, https://web.colby.edu/cogblog/2020/11/24/moving-from-autopilot-towards-mindfulness/.

Part IV. 25–1: Achieving Greatness

1   Adam Grant, *Hidden Potential: The Science of Achieving Greater Things* (Penguin Random House, 2023), 75.

2   Altucher, *Skip the Line*, 165.

3   Jim Kwik, "My Morning Routine (How to Jumpstart Your Brain & Day)," Jim Kwik, May 19, 2017, https://www.jimkwik.com/podcasts/kwik-brain-016-my-morning-routine-how-to-jumpstart-your-brain-day/.

4   Burchard, *High Performance Habits*, 186.

5   Ut Southwestern Medical Center, "Exercise Boosts Blood Flow to the Brain, Study Finds," news release, March 23, 2021, https://www.utsouthwestern.edu/newsroom/articles/year-2021/exercise-boosts-blood-flow-to-the-brain.html.

6   Rebecca Martland et al., "Can High-Intensity Interval Training Improve Mental Health Outcomes in the General Population and Those with Physical Illnesses? A Systematic Review and Meta-Analysis," *British Journal of Sports Medicine* 56, no. 5 (March 2022): 279–291, https://doi.org/10.1136/bjsports-2021-103984.

7   Ming Chang et al., "A Study on Neural Changes Induced by Sauna Bathing: Neural Basis of the 'Totonou' State," *PLoS One* 18, no. 11 (November 2023), https://doi.org/10.1371/journal.pone.0294137.

8   Anne Trafton, MIT News Office, "That Moment When You're Nodding Off Is a Sweet Spot for Creativity," May 15, 2023, news release, https://news.mit.edu/2023/sleep-sweet-spot-dreams-creativity-0515.

9   Anna Steidle and Lioba Werth, "Freedom from Constraints: Darkness and Dim Illumination Promote Creativity," *Journal of Environmental Psychology* 35 (September 2013): 67–80, https://doi.org/10.1016/j.jenvp.2013.05.003.

10 Holiday, *The Obstacle Is the Way*, 57.

11 Will Stone, "Ready to Cold Plunge? We Dive into the Science to See if It's Worth It," NPR, November 20, 2023, https://www.npr.org/sections/health-shots/2023/10/08/1204411415/cold-plunge-health-benefits-how-to.

12 Dale Carnegie, *How to Win Friends and Influence People* (Simon & Schuster, 1936), 221–225.

13 Covey, *The 7 Habits of Highly Effective People*, 289.

14 Julie Smith, *Why Has Nobody Told Me This Before?* (Harper One, 2022).

15 Deepak Chopra and Kabir Sehgal, "3 Science-Backed Ways to Beat the 3 p.m. Slump," CNBC, June 11, 2019, https://www.cnbc.com/2019/06/11/3-science-backed-ways-to-escape-the-afternoon-slump-without-caffeine.html.

16 Howard LeWine, "Does Exercising at Night Affect Sleep?" *Harvard Health Publishing*, July 24, 2024, https://www.health.harvard.edu/staying-healthy/does-exercising-at-night-affect-sleep.

17 Daniel Pink, *When: The Scientific Secrets of Perfect Timing* (Riverhead Books, 2018), 61.

18 Johann Hari, Stolen Focus: Why You Can't Pay Attention—and How to Think Deeply Again (Crown, 2022), 43.

19 Shetty, *Think like a Monk*, 29.

20 Hari, *Stolen Focus*, 66.

21 "Is It Better to Sleep Warm or Cold?," Dr. Mayank Shukla Asthma & Sleep Foundation, accessed September 19, 2025, https://www.drmayankshukla.com/better-sleep-warm-cold/.

22 Danielle Pacheco, "Best Temperature for Sleep," Sleep Foundation, updated July 11, 2025, https://www.sleepfoundation.org/bedroom-environment/best-temperature-for-sleep.

23 Mushtaq, *The Busy Brain Cure*, 98–99.

24 Rose Aschebrock, "Lack of Sleep is Wrecking Your Judgement. Here Are 12 Ways to Get More," Next Big Idea Club, December 11, 2015, https://nextbigideaclub.com/magazine/gretchen-rubin-sleep-is-the-new-sex-12-ways-to-get-more-of-it/1045/.

25 "10 Reasons Why Hydration Is Important," National Council on Aging, January 2, 2025, https://www.ncoa.org/article/10-reasons-why-hydration-is-important.

26 "Talking to Yourself: Is It Normal?," Cleveland Clinic, February 4, 2022, https://health.clevelandclinic.org/is-it-normal-to-talk-to-yourself.

27 Cassie J. Hilditch et al., "Time to Wake Up: Reactive Countermeasures to Sleep Inertia," *Industrial Health* 54, no. 6 (May 2016: 528–541, https://doi.org/10.2486/indhealth.2015-0236.

28 Jodi Schulz, "Stressed? Peppermind Can Help!," Michigan State University Extension, June 1, 2016, https://www.canr.msu.edu/news/stressed_peppermint_can_help.

29 Clear, *Atomic Habits*, 54.

30 Alix Spiegel, "What Vietnam Taught Us about Breaking Bad Habits," NPR, January 2, 2012, https://www.npr.org/sections/health-shots/2012/01/02/144431794/what-vietnam-taught-us-about-breaking-bad-habits.

31 Isaiah Hankel, interview by Jordan Harbinger, *The Jordan Harbinger Show*, episode 91, "Isaiah Hankel: The Smart Way to Focus and Grow Successful," September 5, 2018, https://www.jordanharbinger.com/isaiah-hankel-the-smart-way-to-focus-and-grow-successful/.

32 Dana R. Carney, Amy J. C. Cuddy, and Andy J. Yap, "Power Posing: Brief Nonverbal Displays Affect Neuroendocrine Levels and Risk Tolerance," *Psychological Science* 21, no. 10 (2010): 1363-68, https://doi.org/10.1177/0956797610383437.

33 Song, *Bending Reality*, 44–45.

34 Ericsson and Pool, *Peak*, 59.

35 Smith, *Why Has Nobody Told Me This Before?*, 168.

36 Keith Ferrazzi, *Never Eat Alone: And Other Secrets to Success, One Relationship at a Time* (Crown Business, 2005), xvi.

37 Smith, *Why Has Nobody Told Me This Before?*, 230.

38 Tolle, *The Power of Now*.

39 Leonardo Pires, "Push Notifications Revenue and Growth Statistics (2024)," SignHouse, updated August 1, 2024, https://usesignhouse.com/blog/push-notifications-stats/.

40 "How Often Do You Agree to an App's Request to Allow Push Notifications?," Statista, January 16, 2025, https://www.statista.com/statistics/791005/allow-app-push-notifications-us-mobile-users-by-age-group/.

41 Timothy Taylor, "Economics of Information Overload: Thoughts from Herb Simon," *Conversable Economist* (blog), August 17, 2015, https://conversableeconomist.com/2015/08/17/economics-of-information-overload-thoughts-from-herb-simon/.

42 Mark Zuckerberg, "Q&A with Mark," Facebook, November 6, 2014, https://www.facebook.com/watch/?v=828790510512059.

43 Shetty, *Think like a Monk*, 139–142.

44 Temple Univeristy, "Temple Study Suggests Dressing Your Best Improves Workplace Productivity," news release, June 1, 2023, https://news.temple.edu/news/2023-06-01/when-you-look-good-you-feel-good-research-shows-you-might-even-be-more-productive.

45 Emma Loewe, "I Tried Huberman's Coffee Rules for 6 Months & This Is What I Learned," Mind Body Green, September 3, 2023, https://www.mindbodygreen.com/articles/huberman-coffee-protocol-i-tried-it.

46 Pink, *When*, 46.

47 Caitlin Tilley, "Exactly How Much Caffeine Will Wake You Up—But Not Lead to a Crash, and When to Drink It, According to Experts," University of Michigan Medical School, January 12, 2024, https://medresearch.umich.edu/research-news/exactly-how-much-caffeine-will-wake-you-not-lead-crash-and-when-drink-it-according-experts.

48 Pink, *When*, 69.

49 Matthew Solan, "The Worst Habits for Your Brain," Harvard Health Publishing, April 1, 2022, https://www.health.harvard.edu/mind-and-mood/the-worst-habits-for-your-brain.

50 Nir Eyal, *Indistractable: How to Control Your Attention and Choose Your Life* (Bloomsbury, 2019).

51 Grant, *Hidden Potential*, 74.